WHY SAY NO WHEN THE WORLD SAYS YES

Resisting Temptation in an Immoral World

ESSAYS ON MORALITY

Compiled by
Randal A. Wright

Deseret Book Company
Salt Lake City, Utah

CONTENTS

AVOIDING TEMPTATION

ED AND PATRICIA PINEGAR

We are engaged in a war! And if we are to survive the conflict, we need to understand the issues of this war. It started in heaven, where we were victors: "And there was war in heaven: Michael and his angels [all of us] fought against the dragon" (Revelation 12:7). That war continues every day here on earth—"for the devil is come down unto you, having great wrath, because he knoweth that he hath but a short time" (Revelation 12:12). And we can conquer here, too.

To be locked in combat with Satan can be scary, but it is part of the eternal plan. The Lord has said, "It must needs be that the devil should tempt the children of men, or they could not be agents unto themselves" (D&C 29:39). Indeed, opposition in all things is a necessary condition of our mortality (see 2 Nephi 2:11).

Why do the challenges of life have to be so hard? After all, we all want to return to our heavenly home and our Heavenly Father. We all would like to avoid the big mistakes in life. Why couldn't this process be made easier? Why does there have to be so much opposition? Our Father explained the purpose of life to Abraham when he said, "And we will

prove them herewith, to see if they will do all things whatsoever the Lord their God shall command them" (Abraham
3:25). We are here to be tested—to see if we will yield to
temptation or if we will listen to the promptings of the Spirit.
It is within our power to grow and become like God or, by
submitting to the persuasions of the devil, surrender our potential and be destroyed by Satan. These are the battle lines.

If the enemy is Satan, how can we best prepare for the
battle? How do we know where the adversary will attack? As
children of God, we want to feel good, be loved, be treated
as adults, and feel self-worth. It is on these needs that Satan
concentrates, offering us counterfeit rewards, preying on our
basic desires, striving to exploit our weaknesses. He apparently knows where we are vulnerable, and he charges into
those areas. President Spencer W. Kimball explained,
"Lucifer and his followers know the habits, weaknesses, and
vulnerable spots of everyone and take advantage of them to
lead us to spiritual destruction" (*The Miracle of Forgiveness*
[Salt Lake City: Bookcraft, 1969], pp. 218–19).

We have all been tempted and we know how temptation
works. Let's say you desperately want an *A* in one of your
classes. To ensure that result, you might be tempted to cheat
on an exam or to copy someone else's homework. Satan must
be pleased when he is able to discover that we have become
so anxious to get something that we are willing to set aside
our values to get it—whether it's an *A* in school, some article
out of a store, an immoral experience, or anything else. When
we speak of Satan and his servants throwing their fiery darts
at us, we mean they are trying to deceive us—to convince us
that committing a sin will give us an advantage or make us
feel good. For instance, do you so desperately want to be
accepted that you will seek membership in a gang even though

the cost may be dishonest or violent behavior? Or, in order to feel more important yourself, are you tempted to gossip and find fault with others? Do you want so much to be admired that you would be willing to steal to obtain nicer clothes or a hot car? Do you so much hate being lonely that you might sacrifice eternal values and seek acceptance by joining the crowd in drinking or doing drugs? Or do you want so much to feel appreciated and loved that you would consider accepting an invitation to "go all the way"?

Beware—when you want something "so bad," it usually isn't "so good."

Satan specializes in deception. One of his tactics is to make what is bad, appear good. We also need to be aware that if he discovers any weakness in us—such as pride, selfishness, greed, lust, jealousy, fear, hypocrisy, vanity, apathy, ignorance, or anger—he will try to tempt us in those areas. And, being human, we also suffer from a natural tendency towards sinful behavior. We learn from Moses 5:13 that "they [mankind] loved Satan more than God. And men began from that time forth to be carnal, sensual, and devilish." Those are characteristics we need to resist and overcome.

What are the consequences of yielding to the temptations of Satan? In the end, the fruits are always bitter, no matter how enticing the sin may be made to appear. For instance, those who are tempted to use alcohol or drugs may anticipate a pleasant experience. What results instead are such things as reckless behavior, health risks, trouble with the law, and an unpleasant hangover. The illicit sexual behavior portrayed so often today in literature, music videos, advertisements, and movies is seldom played out far enough to show the pregnancies, abortions, diseases, divorces, and unhappiness that so often follow. The truth is, there is no happiness in wickedness. In fact, the scriptures say that "wickedness *never was* happiness" (Alma 41:10; emphasis added).

Can Satan fulfill our real needs? Will he stand by us, support us, and love us? Korihor put his trust in the devil and then confessed when his evil scheme failed, "The devil hath deceived me" (Alma 30:53). Being abandoned by Satan, Korihor descended into a wretched condition and was finally "run upon and trodden down, even until he was dead." Alma's commentary on this sad episode might serve as an epitaph for Korihor and everyone else who thinks Satan has any loyalty to his disciples. "And thus we see that the devil will not support his children at the last day, but doth speedily drag them down to hell" (Alma 30:60).

The war is on. Satan is real. He attacks, but we have the upper hand. We have the means to defend ourselves; we know how to prepare ourselves, how to avoid the fiery darts of temptation by putting on the armor of Christ (see Ephesians 6:12–17). We do this by making our will and the Lord's will the same — by choosing what he would want us to choose, doing what he would want us to do, saying what he would want us to say.

In this battle we have a leader — the Lord Jesus Christ. Will we listen to this commander? Of course! If we really believe that this earthly war is real, we will listen to and follow him and his servants. We will humbly and gratefully submit to his will and guidance. We will plead and pray for his direction. We will obey just as the Sons of Helaman did — with exactness — and receive the blessings of obedience which are safety and happiness.

The Savior, our leader, knows we can win this war. He and our Heavenly Father have great confidence in us. And they have promised us great blessings. James assures us,

"Blessed is the man that endureth temptation: for when he is tried, he shall receive the crown of life, which the Lord hath promised to them that love him" (James 1:12). Speaking of Abraham, Isaac, and Jacob, the Lord said, "And because they did none other things than that which they were commanded, they have entered into their exaltation, according to the promises, and sit upon thrones, and are not angels but are gods" (D&C 132:37).

President Gordon B. Hinckley has said this of the youth of the Church: "I have great confidence in our young people as a whole. I regard you as the finest generation in the history of the Church. I compliment you, and I have in my heart a great feeling of love and respect and appreciation for you" ("A Chosen Generation," *Ensign,* May 1992, p. 69). Power and strength will come to us when we know and understand the great love, confidence, and trust our leaders have in us.

As we take charge of our battles, what are the attributes we will need in order to overcome the temptations of Satan? Our Heavenly Father and the Savior want us to have the attributes that will give us strength. They know that if we are prayerful, humble, teachable, obedient, and charitable, we can gain self-control, self-mastery, and become responsible — that we can be courageous in defending eternal values; that we can be full of faith and full of the love of Christ; that we can be knowledgeable in the word of God and love that word; that we can be slow to anger and capable of bridling our tongues and our passions. They know we can do it. But we ourselves must learn that we can do it.

These attributes can be ours when we submit to the will of the Father, when we seek to do *his* will, not our will. That is the act of becoming humble, the beginning virtue of all spiritual growth. The battle of "my will" versus "the Lord's will" is the battle of overcoming temptation and yielding to the Spirit of the Lord.

The Lord will validate us by the Spirit when we strive to take upon ourselves these Christlike attributes. Our needs will be met, we will feel good, we'll have a desire to do good — to do justly, to walk humbly, to judge righteously, to be enlightened, to feel joy, to be happy, to have faith. We will feel this approving power in our lives, because we will be accepted of God. Self-worth and self-respect will be ours. Our needs and wants will be met as we conform our needs to the will of our Father. This power will help us win the war.

What specific things can we do to prepare for the battle to resist temptation? What are the Christlike attributes that will help us withstand the buffetings of Satan? We can fortify ourselves and gain these attributes by practicing or experimenting on the word of God and by obeying his commandments. Let us not be deceived by the simplicity of the steps that can bring so much power to our lives.

PRAY

Prayer is a powerful behavior that will fortify us. "Pray always, lest you enter into temptation and lose your reward" (D&C 31:12). We must talk to our Heavenly Father, confide in him, and plead for his help. He will give us direction, encouragement, and power; and in his strength we can do all things. When a young man or young woman kneels in private prayer before going on a date, asking for strength to be pure, he or she is building a powerful fortification.

STUDY THE SCRIPTURES

Studying the scriptures and applying them to our lives will also fortify us. Speaking of the word of God, Alma said that it "had [a] more powerful effect upon the minds of the people than the sword, or anything else" (Alma 31:5). The word of God has power to lead us, guide us, and direct us. The scriptures are our Liahona (see Alma 37:37–47). The word of God, displayed on the Liahona, directed Lehi's family through the wilderness. As they acted with faith and diligence and gave heed to the word, they were directed in all things. Through scripture study we hold to the iron rod, which will guide us through the mists of darkness and the temptations of Satan. Scripture study will be a fortress around us as we study and apply the scriptures to our lives and nurture the word of God through faith, diligence, and patience. A caring mother feels peace when she walks by her child's room and sees her child studying the scriptures. She knows that the power of the word will fortify her daughter.

SERVE

Service can protect us from the adversary. As we nurture and bless others, we are nurtured and blessed by Heavenly Father and strengthened by his Spirit. As we focus on others and try to serve them, our selfishness and personal wants will decrease. We rarely see an unhappy person who is serving with all his heart. That is why missionaries are so blessed — they are continually serving others.

ATTEND CHURCH

Another behavior that will fortify us is church attendance. By attending our meetings, we receive strength through renewing our covenants and learning the word of God. Being in the right place at the right time will strengthen us.

LEARN OBEDIENCE

The word of God teaches us to be obedient, a powerful attribute to experiment on. In his great address, King Benjamin taught, "I would desire that ye should consider on the blessed and happy state of those that keep the commandments of God" (Mosiah 2:41). That verse further advises us, "And if they hold out faithful to the end they are received into heaven, that thereby they may dwell with God in a state of never-ending happiness." Obedience is freedom. When we obey God, we are free from the sins of the world, free from the terrible consequences of sin.

How can we be free with so many rules and commandments to obey? A simple story will illustrate the value of such guidelines.

A little boy and his dad purchased a beautiful kite. Never having flown a kite before, the little boy was excited. The day was perfect. They found an open field. They wound the ball of twine around a stick so the boy could hold on to it, and then they ran, pulling the kite behind them. Finally the wind caught the kite, and it started to fly.

Then they stood still, holding the kite against the wind, and letting out more string. The kite responded by ascending higher and higher. It was exciting, and the little boy was delighted.

After a long while they came to the end of the string, and as they watched the kite, now only a tiny speck in the sky, the little boy suddenly said, "Let's let it go. I want it to be free. I want it to go higher and higher, clear up to Heavenly Father."

The dad replied, "It doesn't work that way, Son. If we let it go, it won't go higher. It will fall instead."

The little boy didn't believe him because the tension on

the string made it seem like the string was holding the kite down. To demonstrate what would happen, the dad opened his pocket knife and handed it to his son. The little boy cut the string. In moments, just moments, the kite lost control. It darted here and there, down and down, and soon they had to walk a long way even to find it, a broken heap on the ground.

The little boy couldn't understand. The string had seemed to be holding the kite down. But it wasn't. The string provided an anchor for the kite, without which it lost its ability to fly.

Like the little boy, some of us mistakenly assume that commandments, rules, and values restrict us — that if we were only free of them, we would be liberated. The truth is, the guidelines provide the discipline that will ultimately lift and guide us to our Heavenly Father. Without the commandments, we would be left to drift aimlessly and eventually crash in a broken heap. As we develop personal, private, religious behavior in the form of prayer, scripture study, service, church attendance, and obedience, we strengthen ourselves against sin and accumulate the power we need to be victorious in our war against Satan.

COMMIT TO FOLLOW TRUE VALUES

One effective strategy we can use in fighting this war is to commit ourselves to true values before the battle ensues — before the crisis, before the moment of confrontation, before the actual temptation. Then, when we need the strength, we won't have to expend our energies in making decisions. That is the principle Joshua sought to teach his people when he counseled, "Choose you *this day* whom ye will serve" (Joshua 24:15; emphasis added). Once these values are firm in our hearts, then we can respond with conviction and determination. Making decisions ahead of the moment of crisis helps us to resist temptations when they are presented.

An example of how this strategy works may be found in the experience of a young boy who early in his life had made a promise to God that he would never do anything to hurt his mother. Later, after he had grown older, he had made another promise that he would never do anything to offend God. Armed with that dual determination he was eventually confronted with a significant temptation.

His high school football team had won a game, and the players and some other fellows had gathered at a house where they were basking in the joy of victory. When one of the boys asked if he could have a drink of water, the host of the party invited him to help himself. Opening the kitchen cupboard to get a glass, he noticed a bottle of cooking wine on a shelf.

"Hey, you guys. Look what I've found! It's almost full! Let's see what wine really tastes like."

With their curiosity aroused and being in a jubilant mood, many of the boys exclaimed, "Yeah, let's do it!"

Only one boy expressed any reservation. "Hey, guys, we shouldn't do this. It isn't right, and besides, the wine isn't ours. You know darn well we shouldn't do this."

Then the abuse began. "What are you, a goody-goody? Hey, flake off, man. We don't need you telling us what to do."

The young man now had to make a decision. "If I drink it, I'll be their pal. If I don't, they'll make fun of me."

Just then he noticed a boy standing in the doorway. The boy was younger, a deacon in the ward where he was a priest. Recalling the promises he had already made — to his God and to his mother — the older boy put his arm around the younger boy's shoulders and said, "Come on, we don't belong here."

They walked away with taunts ringing in their ears but feeling satisfied that they had chosen to do what was right.

You have to wonder what the outcome might have been had the priest not internalized his values and made a decision prior to the temptation—before the moment of crisis.

The most important battle in this war is the one being waged over sexual purity. The Lord has made it clear that we should not engage in sexual transgressions; moreover, even our minds and thoughts should be pure. "Whosoever looketh on a woman, to lust after her, hath committed adultery already in his heart" (3 Nephi 12:28). To lust is to have an unlawful burning desire for, an eagerness to possess, or a yearning to enjoy carnal pleasure. Lust is more than a passing, fleeting thought. It is a thought dwelt on so often that it becomes an emotion or desire that leads to action. Lust is a very common sin in the world, and if we don't guard against it, such temptations can become very real in our lives. The safeguards are to learn to bridle our passions, to control our thoughts, and to focus on the Christlike virtues that can shore us up against this devastating sin.

President Spencer W. Kimball related an experience to illustrate this principle:

"Across the desk sat a handsome nineteen-year-old and a beautiful, shy but charming, eighteen-year-old. They appeared embarrassed, apprehensive, near-terrified. He was defensive and bordering on belligerency and rebellion. There had been sexual violations throughout the summer and intermittently since school began, and as late as last week. . . . Finally the boy said, 'Yes, we yielded to each other, but we do not think it wrong because we love one another.' . . .

"As I looked the boy in the eye, I said, 'No, my boy, you

were not expressing love when you took her virtue.' And to her I said, 'There was no real love in your heart when you robbed him of his chastity. It was lust that brought you together in this most serious of all practices short of murder. . . . ' I continued, 'If one really loves another, one would rather die for that person than injure him. At the hour of indulgence, pure love is pushed out one door while lust sneaks in the other' " (*Faith Precedes the Miracle* [Salt Lake City: Deseret Book Co., 1973], pp. 151–52).

Yes, this war is real, and the consequences of sin are real. Sexual sin is destructive in many ways. It causes the loss of the Spirit, the loss of self-esteem and self-worth; it mocks the power of creation, makes of us seekers of pleasure, and entices us to violate the commandments of God.

As we experiment on the word of God and fortify ourselves with spiritual activities, we may be inspired to do some practical things that will help us avoid temptation:

1. Set your goals, plans, and acceptable behavior early in your life.

2. Remember the Savior in Gethsemane or on the cross.

3. Visualize yourself in the temple dressed in white.

4. Avoid wearing immodest clothing.

5. Avoid going beyond simple expressions of affection.

6. Avoid spending extended periods of time in dangerous places, especially in parked cars.

7. Set a curfew with your parents and your dates and then stick to it.

8. Seek to bless and protect others from immoral behavior.

You can add to this list those things that work for you.

In all things, we must be seekers of happiness (see Alma 27:18) and not simply go with the flow or just have fun—

acting on no values, no plans, no intent to do righteousness. President Ezra Taft Benson has said, "When it comes to the law of chastity, it is better to prepare and prevent than it is to repair and repent" ("The Law of Chastity," address delivered at Brigham Young University, Provo, Utah, 13 Oct. 1987).

Some of us may nevertheless make mistakes. Some will sin. We may even lose a battle. But we never have to lose the war, thanks to the great gift of repentance. Where we are at this moment is important, but the direction we are headed is even more crucial to our success. If we have faith unto repentance, we can overcome and progress toward perfection. We humans on the earth are not perfect, so how do we become just men and women made perfect? Through perfect repentance. The gift of repentance through the atonement of Jesus Christ is the path by which it is possible to gain exaltation—to win our war against Satan. It is not easy to repent, but it is the only way we can win the war. Repentance is the key, and when we repent we fortify ourselves and strengthen ourselves, by the power of God, against future temptation. So we must start where we stand, never minding the past, just learning from it.

What might help us to remember the standards the Lord has given us? Moroni used the Title of Liberty to remind his people. What can we do to make sure we keep the commandments? How can we avoid temptation? Perhaps we can make ourselves little reminders, like a note on the mirror with the simple word *Remember*. What might that word do for us? Reading it, you could "remember" the goodness of God in your life, "remember" to keep the commandments, "remember" to be thankful for all things, "remember" to do good to all mankind, "remember" that upon the rock of Christ we are built— "remember, remember." Just a little word to remind us.

Or maybe a penny placed in our shoe might help us to remember: "I am a daughter or a son of God. I have the capacity to become like Father. I want to be good. I'll remember to pray."

You might associate the ringing of the bell at school or of the telephone at home with your determination to remain virtuous. Whenever you hear that ringing, you can think, "Remember who you are. Remember who you can become. Remember to be kind and good. Remember to tell Mom and Dad you love them. Remember to pray. Remember to search the scriptures."

Remember is the key. Maybe a note written to yourself and left in your car or in your purse or wallet might say, "Remember: Do as Jesus would do." When you rise in the morning and kneel down to pray, you can ask, "Who can I bless today?" There are many other reminders you can use, such as your watch (it's time to choose the right) or even your CTR ring.

Think. Think about what you want out of life. Think about how you will feel if you should slip. Think about how you will feel if you are unworthy to go on a mission or to get married in the temple. Now think about what a wonderful thing it will be to enter marriage worthily, without having sinned. Think about how it will be to kneel at the altar if you are clean and virtuous. You can do it! Others have, and so can you.

HOW MANY KISSES?

—

RAND H. PACKER

When I was thirteen, my friend who was fourteen asked me, "Rand, you kissed a girl yet?"

"Are you kidding?" I responded with a mixture of pride and embarrassment. "I haven't even been out with a girl yet, let alone kissed one. Have you?"

"Yeah," my friend said with cool candor. "Last night, me and Ruth Ann."

"Really? Well, what was it like? How did it go? How did it feel?"

All my friend could say was, "WOW!" Just, "WOW!"

It didn't take me long to discover that my friend was having a "WOW" experience with every girl he went out with. It was kind of a personal challenge to him, something that was expected or even required before a date could be called successful.

You are aware, are you not, that there are some, perhaps many, young men and women who believe that the whole purpose of a date is to get a kiss or even more?

That reminds me of a story about a guy named Bill. He had a date with a girl named Mickie, and when she refused to give him a good-night kiss, he said, "Look, Mickie.

Ordinarily I can understand being refused a good-night kiss on the first date, but this was the junior prom! The ticket cost me twenty dollars, and the flowers were twelve dollars and ten cents."

She wasn't impressed, so he continued. "The tux rental was thirty bucks, and the spot-remover cost me two dollars and ten cents."

Mickie only looked at him a little sorrowfully, and so he babbled on.

"The taxi ride to dinner was eight dollars and three cents, and the dinner was thirty-five dollars and eighty-three cents!"

Not getting the response he wanted, Bill began to scream. "Refreshments were four dollars and eighty-five cents, and the taxi home was nine dollars and thirty-two cents!"

"So," Mickie asked coolly, "What's your point?"

"Well," Bill said plaintively, "Don'tcha think I deserve just a little something?"

So she wrote him out a check for one hundred twenty-two dollars and twenty-three cents.

It is obvious that the only thing Bill was interested in that night was not Mickie's happiness but a selfish gratification of his own physical desires. Mickie's feelings seemed to mean nothing to Bill, for which she paid him back with equal warmth: a cold check for $122.23.

What is a kiss worth, anyway? Better still, what is a kiss for? And what does a kiss do?

Obviously, one effect of kissing is that it stirs the passions that exist in all of us. Those passions were put there by a loving Father whose intent is to help us become like him. The emotions, passions, and desires that are part of our physical makeup are not illegitimate but rather important characteristics that will help us fulfill our ultimate destiny. The

Lord has told us that until we are properly married, we are to control these passions. Then, after we are married, we can enjoy the expression of them and they will serve to bring us and our spouse closer together and ultimately make us "one"—both physically and spiritually.

It is interesting that one of the words meaning "kiss" in the Hebrew language is *nasaq,* which also means "to catch fire" or "to burn or kindle." But this kindling must be done on the Lord's timetable, or the entire forest is in danger of being burned to the ground and left desolate for at least a season. The passions themselves are God-given, hence the commandment, "And also see that ye bridle all your passions, that ye may be filled with love" (Alma 38:12).

The purpose of a bridle is to control and to keep headed in the right direction. A horse without a bridle is like a run-away freight train with no track. I have been on the back of a galloping runaway horse without a bridle, hanging on for dear life and having no control of where I was being taken. If I had only had a bridle, I could have controlled the horse. Instead, he controlled me and dumped me at his own pleasure.

The media has helped convince the world that a kiss is an expression of passion and a prelude to sexual behavior. No longer is it a symbol of loyalty, pure affection, and respect. Merchants intent on selling their wares promise us that if we will just chew their brand of gum, wear their style of clothing, soak ourselves in their sensuous fragrance, drive their make of car, or visit their recommended vacation spot, they can get us kisses. In fact, they imply, they can get us a whole lot more than kisses.

If there is mutual attraction, it is natural for a young man and a young woman to enjoy spending time together. If they do not take care to structure the amount of time they spend and control the places they go together, they are likely to become improperly affectionate with each other. As surely as night follows day, prolonged kissing leads to more intimate expressions — expressions that the Lord has commanded us to reserve for the beautiful and sacred relationship of husband and wife. Kissing soon gives way to necking, kindling the flame of desires more intensely. Necking is defined as passionate kissing, which includes French kissing or "soul kissing," as it is often called. It is easy to see the relationship of such kissing to total sexual expression.

As desires are stoked, petting often ensues. Petting involves the touching and fondling of private, sacred parts of the body and is itself a forbidden sexual activity for single people. It carries a restriction imposed by Heavenly Father, stamped in bold letters, **"For Married Couples Only!"**

The passions unleashed by this kind of intimacy are so powerful that once they are ignited — like gasoline being splashed on a fire — they become increasingly difficult to control. Those who stimulate themselves in this way — whether innocently or by design — are flirting with unhappy consequences. Many young people have broken their own hearts and forfeited their blessings by foolishly imagining they could trifle with these sacred emotions or use them for recreational purposes.

The sharing of oneself with another in this way is part of the process of becoming "one" with each other. Though it is a physical relationship, it overflows with spiritual implications. There really is no other experience in life quite like it. To give oneself in this way is to give all that one is and ever hopes to be, to someone else. But, this giving requires permission and authority from the great giver of life Himself.

How can the sexual activity that is so destructive before marriage be a sanctifying experience in the marriage? Why does the Lord condone and bless sexual activity after marriage and condemn it before?

Over the course of my life I have had reason to counsel with many unmarried young people who said they loved each other. These couples often ask me, "Why is it so wrong to show our love? We're going to be married anyway. Why is sharing our love in this way evil prior to a ceremony and celestial after some words have been said? How does a ceremony or a signed piece of paper change all that?" These are important questions and deserve to be answered.

If you were to have walked down the streets of Jerusalem in the days of Jesus, you would have noticed certain individuals walking toward you with large keys tied around their neck. The keys were evidence that there was a room somewhere in which great wealth or something of value was stored. The key entitled the bearer to enter the room and to partake of its contents. The only legitimate access to the room was by use of the key. To safeguard the key and reduce the possibility of the keys being stolen, they were secured around the owner's neck. Hence the imagery of "keys," which was often used by the Savior. Certainly thieves could break into the room and steal the riches and wealth. But someday they would be found out and made to pay for their crime, either in this life or the next. The purpose of the key was not only to protect the wealth but to unlock the wealth, making it available to be used.

Even today, keys play a vital role. Outside my office in the parking lot is a little Chevrolet Chevette. Underneath the hood are about forty idle horses not doing anything. Each night I walk out to my car, insert my key, and unleash the power of those forty idle horses, turning them into anxious thoroughbreds ready to take me to my destination. Yes, someone could break into the car, hot wire it, and steal it. But again, sometime, either in this life or the next, the truth will be known and payment exacted.

It is my belief that when a young couple goes to the temple, they receive a celestial key (permission) to use their procreative powers. That is a first step in our journey toward godhood. The marriage ceremony is the way the Lord officially sanctions the right to touch each other, to share ourselves, and to join with God in the creation of life.

It may be useful to think of the physical relationship between a man and a woman as God's gift to the marriage and that we are not to open the present early. I have discovered that after twenty-two years of marriage, all of our original wedding presents, so far as I know, have vanished — except God's gift to our marriage. It remains with us still and will forever. There is nothing quite like this gift.

If we follow our Father's instructions in this matter, the promise is a greater glory, "which glory shall be a fulness and a continuation of the seeds forever and ever" (D&C 132:19). To me this promise means that someday, after my sweetheart and I have learned all that we are supposed to learn, Heavenly Father might say to us, "Rand and Shirlee, go over there about three hundred twenty-nine light years, veer to the left for another seventy-two light years, and then you can be together forever and ever and have a relationship with each other forever and ever and have quarterbacks and cheerleaders forever and ever." I know of no promise that God has given that thrills me more than this one.

If you are still confused about premarital sex or if you are struggling with temptation, consider this. Those who wait until after marriage to share physical intimacies are not only free to discover the pleasure but, unencumbered by guilt, are able to enjoy an astonishing, glorious, and joyful experience. On the other hand, those who elect not to wait forfeit something precious and always describe the experience as being somehow empty, hollow, and disappointing.

We have now come full circle in regard to the question we asked in the beginning about when and with whom to share kisses. The relationship between a man and a woman can be either good or bad, and the starting point of that relationship is a kiss. When should you share a kiss, and where? How many dates before a kiss is appropriate? Is kissing bad? Is it okay to kiss before you are married? Perhaps this little story will provide some answers.

THE KISS

Not even in Camelot were there evenings such as this — evenings undoubtedly created for fireflies to do their magic. Like tiny candles, a trillion little flecks of light danced in the fragrant darkness of the palace garden.

A soft hand reached gently into the night and with a velvet grasp held captive a single and frightened flicker.

"Would you like a glimpse into another world?" asked the princess as she brought her hands close to his eyes. The young knight, Sir Jason of Lockton, peered into the darkness of her cupped hands, his eyes chasing every zigzag of the captive dancing flicker. Suddenly, without warning, the princess released her lighted prisoner, and the little creature darted heavenward to conceal itself in the pattern of glittering stars.

"Father always used to call me his little firefly," said the princess as she stared into the darkness.

"Jenny the Firefly," quipped Jason. "I like it. I really like it."

"Oh, I can tell," laughed Jenny. "You mock my father."

"On the contrary," said Jason. "I judge your father correct. Why else is he the king? His wisdom is much greater than his years, and his daughter much more fair to look upon than the clouds at sunrise."

"Jenny the Cloud," smiled the princess. "I like that. I really like that. It has a kind of billowy ring to it, doesn't it?"

"Now you mock me," said Jason. "I've looked forward to this evening for many months and finally it is my turn."

"Turn?" questioned Jenny.

"The knights of the kingdom, Jenny. You know they stand in line to be your escort. I may not get another turn until the March winds blow."

"I see," said the princess. "But, if you are different from them, might I invite you back on the morrow?"

"Oh, if only you would, Jenny. If only you would," pleaded the young knight.

The reflecting pond shimmered as the soft evening breeze wended its way through the palace garden. For the young knight this hour had been a long time coming, and his wait had seemed eternal. With excitement he had anticipated this special moment. The setting was right — a palace garden, fragrant night air, twinkling stars, flickering fireflies, a young knight, and a not so typical run-of-the-palace princess. She controlled not only her own destiny but the destiny also of this young knight. They grew silent as they stood beside the statue of El Tibaar, a monument to the king's faithful and proven steed.

"Now is the time," thought Sir Jason to himself. "This is the moment I have been waiting for and dreaming about."

His heart was pounding as he closed his eyes and leaned forward to kiss the object of his desire, anticipating the feel of her lips. But the princess closed not her eyes, and dipping her head gracefully to the side, she watched as the knight laid his lips squarely on the nose of El Tibaar. Feeling the cold, lifeless rock, Jason instantly opened his eyes to find himself staring at the nose of an ungiving and stone-cold horse.

"Do you have no regard for my feelings?" the princess gently chided. "That which you want you cannot take, nor can I give to all. The days of our acquaintance are but few and this our first night. Is there not more for us than the conquest of a kiss?"

A look of despair and defeat came over Jason, and the young warrior and future king retreated, vanishing into the night with heavy thought as his only companion.

For several moments Jenny stared into the night and at a trillion fireflies. Suddenly all was blurry as tears welled to overflowing. She bolted toward the privacy of her chamber, running to beat the flood of emotion that threatened to overwhelm her. As she approached the sloping stairs that would deliver her to the comfort of the castle, a strong pair of hands suddenly reached out from the darkness, and she was held captive.

She cried out in fear.

"Princess, Princess, 'tis I," said the king. "Be not afraid."

"Oh, Father, you startled me so," said Jenny as she relaxed into his protective arms and buried her face deep in his kingly robe, hoping to hide the moist evidence of a miserable night.

"What are you doing out here?" she asked.

"That's the question I'm supposed to ask," countered

King Rourke, good-naturedly. "I suppose it is permissible for the king to walk in his own garden, is it not? I was merely standing here when I was nearly trampled by a certain young knight heading somewhere in great haste. I didn't know that you were that ferocious, my little. . . "

"Oh, Father," Jenny blurted out. "How do you know when it's right to kiss someone, and why is it that almost every young knight who takes my hand thinks that a kiss is his just reward for an evening of gallantry?"

"Ah," sighed the king. "Two very large questions, very large indeed. Perhaps the answer to your first question will allow you to control the second."

"Is there an answer, Father?" asked Jenny.

"There is, my princess, there is. I remember the first time my eyes beheld your mother. Ah, she was as pure as she was beautiful. Not even the first snows of winter were purer than she. Oh, how I longed to kiss her, to take her in my arms and hold her close. But somewhere, I know not where, I had learned that when a kiss is given, it must be not only mine but 'ours.' There is an eternal meaning attached to a kiss, Jenny, and there are precious few who understand the real meaning."

"But how did you know that Mother felt the same way? How did you know that it was right to give it, and how many times do you give it, and to how many people? I'm so confused."

"Welcome to the world, Princess. Confusion reigns. But it need not. There are answers. Somewhere in this old king's study is the answer to your question."

"You mean you have a book on kissing?"

"Sort of," smiled the king. "And besides, I've been doing it for years. I'm pretty good, you know."

"Really, Father? It seems so funny to hear you talk this way. I can't imagine you ever kissing or even being young enough to feel what I'm feeling. The way I'm going, I may be the only maiden in the kingdom never to have kissed."

"Well, there's one thing that I'm pretty sure of, my little firefly: if you save all of your kisses for the one you're going to marry, you probably will never find one to marry, knowing young men as I do, mind you."

Jenny opened her eyes wide, and she smiled thinly, puzzled by her father's statement. Then, arm in arm, the princess and her father ascended the steps to the king's library.

That room had always been a little frightening to Jenny. It was there that many great decisions were made concerning the kingdom. Jenny had sometimes peeked in and had overheard the solemn conversations between powerful people. But tonight it was quiet in the study, and there was an almost spiritual feeling in the room.

"Somewhere, up there, Jenny, is a book, a special book."

Jenny peered above the king's head at the rows of bound volumes, their titles illuminated by the dim light cast by a single candle.

"Ah, there it is. I think I see it, Jenny. That's got to be it."

Jenny watched with interest as her father drew from the topmost shelf an old, tattered, large, leather-bound book. Though the volume had obviously once been well used, it was now covered with dust. Holding it reverently, the king gently brushed away the evidence of a dozen years of neglect.

Laying the huge volume on his marble-topped desk, Rourke opened the heavy book and began to search its pages.

Jenny's eyes registered great surprise. "Father? That is

holy writ you touch. Is not the vicar the only one authorized to read the words of life? You stand condemned by your own decree."

"Shhhh," quieted the king. "A foolish tradition, Jenny, started ages ago by some foolish prince of darkness. I am bound by senseless law to abide the decree, but someday, when light fills the earth, all will have the words of life and answers to questions."

Finally the king's eyes rested on a single page. Then, looking up, he said, "Long ago, the greatest of kings stood in the midst of rabble as the events of a very sacred evening were intruded upon. The traitor came in the company of evil men and made his way hesitantly toward the king. There, with a kiss, he betrayed him.

"Do you know who I am talking about?" Rourke asked his daughter.

"Yes," smiled Jenny. " 'Tis our Lord and Savior."

"That's right, Jenny. Now listen to his response to the treachery and try to imagine the pain he must have felt."

" 'Judas, betrayest thou the Son of man with a kiss?' It was not the betrayal that hurt the Savior that night, Jenny. He knew that was going to happen. It was the symbol of affection Judas chose to work his evil that hurt the great King so. It was the kiss — a symbol of love, devotion, caring, loyalty, protection, and commitment. Perhaps, Jen, if you think about the meaning of a kiss and what it should represent, it will help you know who to kiss and when. To distribute or collect kisses for mere physical pleasure betrays the true and total meaning of what a kiss is meant to be. The kiss is yours, Princess. It cannot be taken; it can only be given."

Rourke gently closed the sacred volume and looked into the eyes of his precious daughter.

"You know what, Jen? There are few knights in the kingdom who would understand what we have just talked about. To a true knight that understanding will come, but for now he is mostly enthralled with the beauty that he sees and with how it makes him feel."

Jenny gazed silently at the volume on the desk.

"Does that book always have answers like that, Father?"

"Most of the time, Princess, if you are willing to search them out. Now, run along. The hour is late. Just remember that there is precious more to a kiss than kindling a fire within you, although that's an important part too. Keep in mind the beautiful and sacred things a kiss symbolizes, and you'll know when and with whom to share it."

Jenny threw her arms around her father and gave him a hug fit for a king.

"Thank you for being here and listening. Are you always this wise, Father?"

"Always," said Rourke, winking affectionately at his beautiful daughter and holding the book next to his heart. "Always."

CONTROLLING YOUR THOUGHTS

DAVID A. CHRISTENSEN

I had an experience a number of years ago that affected my life and the life of a young missionary. My wife and I and our children were living in São Paulo, Brazil, setting up the seminary program. I was also serving as a member of the mission presidency.

In an emergency, I was called to be the acting mission president of the Brazil São Paulo Central Mission. I was given the challenge to work with 185 missionaries, as well as to try to keep the seminary program going. My wife and I found it a great challenge but a very rewarding one.

As the acting mission president, I had the demanding but enjoyable task of interviewing all the missionaries. One of these interviews made a lasting impression on me. A missionary came into my office. He was a handsome young man. The elder had a wonderful spirit about him, and he was a hard worker. But at the end of the interview he said to me, "President, I have something I would like to talk over with you, if I may." I invited him to tell me the problem and said I would help as much as I could. Then he said, "President, I have a hard time controlling my thoughts, and sometimes they become dirty. I want to be able to stop thinking those kinds of thoughts because they prevent me from having the Spirit of the Lord like I'd like to."

He had been assigned to labor in a very difficult area of the mission, a section of the city near the ocean front in one of the tourist regions. To reach their proselyting area, he and his companion often had to walk along streets bordering the beach. There was a great temptation to look at the sunbathers and swimmers and to think improper thoughts. Because he and his companion were obviously American, they received admiring glances from many attractive young women who sought occasion to walk by them. My young missionary friend said, "President, it's so difficult for me. I try to do so well, but when these young women parade themselves in front of me, I find my mind filled with inappropriate thoughts, and I am having a very difficult time controlling them." The elder was obviously deeply repentant and sorrowful, and he earnestly desired to do the work of the Lord and to keep himself clean and pure, both in thought and deed.

I said to him, "Elder, tell me what you're doing to overcome your problem?" He told me that he had confessed his sins to his Heavenly Father, that he daily sought help from the Lord, and that he had come to talk with me to make sure that his confession was complete. He felt he was doing everything he could to successfully control his inappropriate thoughts. I asked him, "If I teach you a principle, will you live it?" And he said, "I will, President." Together, we opened the Doctrine and Covenants to the forty-third section and read verses 8 and 9: "And now, behold, I give unto you a commandment, that when ye are assembled together ye shall instruct and edify each other, that ye may know how to *act* and direct my church, how to *act* upon the points of my law and commandments, which I have given.

"And thus ye shall become instructed in the law of my church, and be sanctified by that which ye have received, and *ye shall bind yourselves to act in all holiness before me*" (emphasis added).

We talked about that scripture and in particular about the last phrase, "ye shall bind yourselves to act in all holiness before me." I said to this fine young missionary, "I have found that whenever we are obedient to the Lord, he blesses us. If you will be obedient to the principle taught in these verses, the Lord will bless you."

And then we talked about how to bind ourselves to the Lord — how to act in all holiness before him. We talked about the meaning of the word *bind*. Bind means to commit, or to covenant, or to promise. Therefore, when we bind ourselves to the Lord we commit to him, or promise him that we will act in all holiness. Then I explained that the most important aspect of that binding is our *recognition* that without his power and strength we cannot accomplish our task, but that with his strength, we can do anything required of us. We talked about the fact that our Father in Heaven has all power, including the power to help us do whatever he requires, whether that might be to proselyte sixteen hours a day or keep our thoughts pure.

The elder promised me that in his morning prayer the next day, he would bind himself to the Lord — that he would commit himself and promise his Heavenly Father that he would do everything in his power to keep his thoughts clean and pure. He promised that when he was tempted to think about something improper, he would immediately put it from his mind. And he promised that he would not intentionally entertain any evil thought. Finally, he agreed that he would plead with his Father in Heaven for strength and power to keep his commitment. He went from my office much encouraged.

I met with him the following evening. When he walked into my office he had a big smile on his face. He seemed a little sheepish as we began our conversation, but he was anxious to explain to me what had happened. He said, "This morning I did as I told you I would do, and I committed myself to Heavenly Father to keep my thoughts clean and pure and to be a worthy servant. I promised him that I would do everything possible to keep my thoughts clean and that when improper thoughts entered my mind I would immediately get rid of them. In addition, I pleaded with Heavenly Father that he would grant me power and strength to keep my commitment, and that I might receive a witness that the promise in the forty-third section of the Doctrine and Covenants was true."

As he and his companion had left their apartment that morning they had to walk near the beach on the way to their tracting area. He was feeling optimistic and happy, but his resolve was soon challenged. A beautiful young woman saw the elders coming and deliberately crossed the street and walked past them.

My young friend then made the fatal Mormon mistake! He said to himself, "I can handle this! I can take one look and still control my mind." So he took a look and found he could *not* control his mind, which was immediately flooded by inappropriate and dirty thoughts. He said, "I felt so bad I wanted to die."

Obviously he could not throw himself down along the beach and raise his arms to heaven and cry out, "Oh Father, forgive me." But as he walked along, suffering the pains and anguish of having broken his promise to the Lord, he prayed in his heart for forgiveness and strength and power to do better. A few minutes later, when he had another opportunity to think inappropriate thoughts, he remembered his promise and kept them clean.

As the young missionary sat with me that evening he said with a big grin, "President, I only blew it a few times today and that's the best I have ever done." He had begun a process that would ultimately change his life, and he became one of the truly great missionaries in that mission because he grasped the great truth taught by Jacob: "Remember, to be carnally-minded is death, and to be spiritually-minded is life eternal" (2 Nephi 9:39).

The principle talked about in Doctrine and Covenants 43:8–9 is one of tremendous importance to every young man and woman in the Church. Obviously, our thoughts precede our actions, and if there were no inappropriate thoughts, there would be no inappropriate actions. For, as the Lord said, "As [a person] thinketh in his heart, so is he" (Proverbs 23:7).

A former president of the Church, George Albert Smith, related a boyhood experience: "As a child, thirteen years of age, I went to school at Brigham Young Academy. . . . I cannot remember much of what was said during the year that I was there, but there is one thing that I will probably never forget. . . . Dr. [Karl G.] Maeser one day stood up and said:

" 'Not only will you be held accountable for the things you do, but you will be held responsible for the very thoughts you think.'

"Being a boy, not in the habit of controlling my thoughts very much, it was quite a puzzle to me what I was to do, and it worried me. In fact, it stuck to me just like a burr. About a week or ten days after that it suddenly came to me what he meant. I could see the philosophy of it then. All at once there came to me this interpretation of what he had said: Why of course you will be held accountable for your thoughts, because when your life is completed in mortality, *it will be the sum of your thoughts.* That one suggestion has been a great blessing to me all my life, and it has enabled me upon many occasions to avoid thinking improperly, because I realize that I will be, when my life's labor is complete, the product of my thoughts" (*Sharing the Gospel with Others* [Salt Lake City: Deseret Book Co., 1948], pp. 62–63).

Each of you who reads this chapter has a great mission to accomplish in the earth. You have a great opportunity to exert your influence not only in the Church but also among your friends who may not be members of the Church. In order to fulfill your mission you'll have to be worthy, and in order to be worthy you will have to learn to control your thoughts.

As you make your morning commitment to your Heavenly Father and as you meet the challenge of controlling your thoughts during the day, you might like to remember a wonderful suggestion made by Elder Boyd K. Packer: "The mind is like a stage. . . . Have you noticed that without any real intent on your part, in the middle of almost any performance, a shady little thought may creep in from the wings and attract your attention? These delinquent thoughts will try to upstage everybody. If you permit them to go on, all thoughts of any virtue will leave the stage. You will be left, because you consented to it, to the influence of unrighteous thoughts. . . .

"This is what I would teach you. Choose from among the sacred music of the Church a favorite hymn, . . . one with words that are uplifting and music that is reverent, one that makes you feel something akin to inspiration. . . .

"Go over it in your mind carefully. Memorize it. Even though you have had no musical training, . . . now, use this hymn as the place for your thoughts to go. Make it your emergency channel. Whenever you find these shady characters have slipped from the sidelines of your thinking onto the stage of your mind, put on this record, as it were" ("Inspiring Music — Worthy Thoughts," *Ensign,* Jan. 1974, p. 28).

This suggestion by Elder Packer has been very helpful in my life. And there are other techniques that you can use to help you keep your commitment to your Father in Heaven. Some youth tell me they have chosen a scripture to memorize that they can recite when it is needed. For myself, I use a very simple technique of talking immediately to my Father in Heaven when such thoughts come into my mind. Or, I talk to myself. For instance, if I'm riding alone in the car, I simply shout out loud, "Get out of there!" Some people may look strangely at me as they go by in their cars, but the battle is between me and Satan, not between me and the passing traffic.

Elder Bruce R. McConkie recommends that we preach a little sermon to ourselves when Satan attempts to plant evil in our minds. Whatever the technique, the important thing is that we have committed ourselves to our Heavenly Father in our morning prayer, that we have pleaded with him for his power and blessing, and that we do everything we can to keep our thoughts pure.

The technique that we use to rid ourselves of evil thoughts is up to us and our own creativity. The Lord has said, "Look unto me in every thought" (D&C 6:36). We can do that. The more fully we learn to control our thoughts, the more capable we will be of doing what Alma counseled us to do — to lift up our thoughts to our Heavenly Father all the day long (see Alma 34).

The Savior's instruction to us is very simple. Speaking of evil things, he said, "Behold, I give unto you a commandment, that ye suffer none of these things to enter into your heart" (3 Nephi 12: 29). Can you imagine how world history might have been changed if men and women had just lived by this principle and had stopped their evil thoughts before they became evil acts?

Because of my name, I have always had a great feeling of love for David of the Old Testament. As a teenager I used to read of his astonishing victory over Goliath and imagine myself doing the same thing. Admiring King David as I did, the story of his illicit relationship with Bathsheba always did (and still does) make me sorrowful. To see one of my heroes lose his exaltation has always been difficult for me. But imagine what *might* have happened if David had just controlled his thoughts. His scriptural story would now read something like this: "And it came to pass in an eveningtide, that David arose from off his bed, and walked upon the roof of the king's house: and from the roof he saw a woman washing herself; and the woman was very beautiful to look upon.

"But David turned himself away and returned unto his house. Yea, and David did sing a hymn; yea, he did quote his favorite scripture. And, behold, he thought no more upon the woman" (see 2 Samuel 11:2–3).

Now, isn't that better? Then Doctrine and Covenants 132:39 would read: "And in none of these things did [David] sin against me . . . and he has [not] fallen from his exaltation." That change would make me so happy! It would also please the Lord. And David would be free to return to his Heavenly Father and to enjoy all the blessings of eternal life.

But we can't change the past. David did not control his thoughts. He did sin with Bathsheba. He did cause the death of Uriah. And he has lost his exaltation. That is the unerasable fact.

Your scriptural story is still being written, however. You can change it if you need to. You and the Lord can bring your thoughts under control. Your whole life is before you!

With all this in mind, can you imagine what you, as one of the youth of Zion, can accomplish for your Father in Heaven and for yourself if you learn to control your thoughts? You can be free from sexual immorality of any kind. You can be free to go on a mission, marry in the temple, and raise a good family. You can also be free to enjoy peace of conscience, revelation, and happiness. But perhaps more than anything else, you can be free to enjoy this wonderful promise made to us by the Lord: "Let virtue garnish thy thoughts unceasingly; then shall thy confidence wax strong in the presence of God; and the doctrine of the priesthood shall distil upon thy soul as the dews from heaven. . . . The Holy Ghost shall be thy constant companion, and thy scepter an unchanging scepter of righteousness and truth" (D&C 121:45–46).

Can you imagine all that? When you learn to control your thoughts and fill your mind with virtue, you have the right to feel confident with Heavenly Father. Your prayers will become better and better. They will be more meaningful. Instead of being a duty, prayer will become a pleasure. You will pray morning and evening because you will *want* to. You will learn to pray with faith. You will get answers to your prayers.

But besides all that, when you feel confident with God, you will also feel confident with those around you, and that's important to your happiness. Zits and pounds and pressures can all come and go, and you'll still be okay. With the constant companionship of the Holy Ghost, your patriarchal blessing will be fulfilled and you will complete the mission for which your Heavenly Father sent you.

Now, I need to warn you of one great danger. As surely as God lives, so does the adversary. He will constantly try to tell you you can't do it. But you can.

Controlling your thoughts (as you are probably already aware) takes time. Some weaknesses can be controlled quickly, but some take a lifetime to overcome. Perhaps controlling your thoughts seems like it will take you a lifetime. But don't get discouraged! Don't give up! Each day can become better. Each week will bring greater control. Each month will see increased strength. Don't let Satan sell you short. You *can* learn to control what runs through your mind. Practice *does* make perfect.

Begin now. Robert Louis Stevenson said something I memorized when I was a teenager. He said, "You cannot run away from weakness. You must sometime fight it out or perish. And if that be so, why not now and where you stand?" That statement has changed my life. It can change yours, too.

MODESTY –
IT'S ALWAYS IN STYLE

JOY SAUNDERS LUNDBERG

At last I was sixteen years old and ready to date. The prom was coming up, and I just had to go! But no one else seemed to notice. I kept waiting to be asked and praying that my dream guy would be the one. Well, he *was* the one . . . for someone else! So my prayer changed to a simple, "Please help somebody ask me . . . anybody!" I wasn't actually feeling quite that desperate, but almost. About a week before the prom my prayer was answered, and someone finally asked me to go with him. He wasn't my dream guy, but he was a nice guy, and I was as excited as a cheerleader just winning the tryouts.

I lived on a farm, and to get home from school I had to ride a bus and then walk another half mile. That day I jumped off the bus and ran that half mile as fast as I could. I could hardly wait to tell my mother about my date. I burst into the kitchen where she was working and shouted, "Mom, I got a date to the prom!" She was really happy for me. My tongue shifted into high gear as I raced on with all the exciting details.

Then I realized something. "Oh, no! Mom, I've got a real problem. I don't have a thing to wear!" My mother is a great mom with lots of talents, but taking a piece of material and turning it into a beautiful formal isn't one of them. And the only job I had was working at home with all the family responsibilities, so I had no way to earn the money to buy myself a dress. I knew I would be asking for money from parents who had little, and I was worried. My dad was a struggling farmer with nine kids. I had asked for things before, and many times the reply had been, "We'd love to, honey, but we just don't have the money." Have you ever experienced that? If you have, then you'll understand how I felt.

Mom said, "I'll talk to Daddy and see what we can do." Later that day Dad came to me and said, "This is really important to you, isn't it?"

"Oh, yes, Daddy. For this purpose I was born."

He got the picture. "Mom's going to take you shopping tomorrow." I threw my arms around his neck and was absolutely certain I had the best dad in the whole world.

So the next day, there Mom and I were, in the middle of a dress shop, surrounded by the latest styles in formal evening wear. Do you know what the latest style was in the fifties? Strapless! Do you know who the prophet was then? David O. McKay, and he had said the very words to us that today's prophet has said to you: "Be modest." And my parents were ultimate, top-of-the-line believers in whatever the prophet said. "Be modest" was ringing in my ears as we looked around. Nothing but strapless. As I stood looking at all those strapless evening gowns hanging there, I thought, "How do they hang there?" Think about it.

In the next dress shop, the same thing – not even an *ugly* gown that covered the shoulders. The third dress shop was the same story. I was completely discouraged. Moreover, I suddenly realized something. If every formal in the stores was strapless, then every girl at the prom would be wearing a strapless dress! At that very moment Satan started up his little song and dance routine on my shoulder. You know how it goes: "Ya wanna be 'in,' . . . ya gotta be 'in.' " And I thought, "Yeah, I want to be 'in.' " That was when I saw it . . . this beautiful, peach-colored evening gown that was so stunning it drew me to it like a magnet.

"Oh, Mom. Look! It's my color," I said. "Well, I *think* it's my color. How about if I try this one on, just to see if I really do look good in this color?" She consented, "But only to see if it's your color."

In the dressing room I slipped it on, zipped it up, and looked in the mirror. You should have seen what I saw looking back at me . . . this gorgeous woman! You wouldn't believe what that dress did for me. I had to have it! I went out to show my mother and said, "Mom, we have looked everywhere, and there just isn't anything but strapless. So, . . . well, . . . I think we're just forced into this purchase."

With a wry smile she replied, "No, we're not. But it is beautiful, and it does come up nice and high. How about if we get some matching material and I make a little covering for your shoulders. Then it would be modest." Knowing there was no other way, I agreed. Soon, we were on our way home with my gorgeous gown and the unwanted extra material.

The next day, before Mom had a chance even to begin making the covering for my shoulders, the phone rang. It was my married brother, Lee, who was living four hundred miles away, attending Brigham Young University. "Guess what?" he said to my mom. "You are now a grandma!" The first grandchild in our family had just been born. My mother was so excited and so needed that in a matter of hours she was on a bus headed to Provo, Utah. In her haste, she forgot all about making the covering for my shoulders. And so did I!

The night of the prom arrived, and Mom was still gone. I spent hours getting ready. My hair was exquisite, and my dress was absolutely celestial. (Whoops! Wrong word.) It was absolutely, stunningly, revealingly. . . strapless. I felt like a beautiful barbie doll, except of course, they didn't exist then. I was so excited.

Fifteen minutes before my date was to arrive, I walked into the living room. Oh, oh. There was my dad! He took one look at me and said, "Where did you get that dress?"

With piety and feigned innocence I replied, "Mother bought it for me."

"Mother would never buy that without a plan. What was the plan?"

"Oh, there was a plan, Daddy. Mother was going to make a covering for my shoulders so I would be modest, but she had to leave, and . . . oh, Daddy . . . I'm just sick about it, but I don't have any choice. I have to go this way."

With a look that penetrated into the center of my soul but offering no reprimand, he simply said, "Get the material . . . and scissors, and a needle, and thread. Quickly!"

I obeyed. As I searched for these items, all I could think of was how I had never seen my daddy sew anything. I was worried.

Without a word, he took the material, held it up, looked at it, laid it on the table, and folded it several times until it was a strip about six inches wide. He brought one end over to the top of my dress and carefully stitched it in place, using little tiny stitches — not the kind you can pull and . . . zip, they're out. No. These were there for the night. Then he wrapped the material around the back and brought the other end forward to the top of my dress on the other side, cut off the excess, and stitched it in place. And *I was modest!* As he finished, I thought, "Tonight is the night I die."

With a smile he said, "You look pretty."

Unconvinced, I went to my room to look in the mirror and check out the damage. To my surprise, it didn't look too bad. Not great, but not bad. The ruffles hid the stitches, thank goodness. Just then there was a knock at the door. It was my date, and off we went to the dance.

As we danced around the floor that night, surrounded by all those bare shoulders, something happened to me. Nobody else knew it happened, but I knew, because it happened inside of me. You see, I began to realize how much my parents really loved me. They loved me enough to insist that I obey the prophet and dress modestly. And I have to confess it felt good.

I don't think anything bad would have happened to me that night if I had gone to the prom with bare shoulders, but the scary part is, I might have really enjoyed being "of the world." After compromising in this area, I might have found it easier to do other things contrary to gospel teachings and, step by step, have been led away from the most important blessing that can come to any of us—temple marriage.

Modesty is an important principle in helping us live to be worthy of the great blessings our Heavenly Father has promised the obedient. In the booklet *For the Strength of Youth* our Church leaders have said: "Servants of God have always counseled his children to dress modestly to show respect for him and for themselves. Because the way you dress sends messages about yourself to others and often influences the way you and others act, you should dress in such a way as to bring out the best in yourself and those around you.

However, if you wear an immodest bathing suit because it's 'the style,' it sends a message that you are using your body to get attention and approval, and that modesty is not important."

It goes on to explain what is *not* modest. "Immodest clothing includes short shorts, tight pants, and other revealing attire. Young women should refrain from wearing off-the-shoulder, low-cut, or revealing clothes. Young men should similarly maintain modesty in their dress. All should avoid tight fitting or revealing clothes and extremes in clothing and appearance" (p. 8).

Are you thinking, "Hey, nobody's going to tell me what I can wear. I'm going to be in style!" Maybe, for example, you just bought a new spandex outfit (talk about "tight fitting!"). When tight clothing such as that is worn, it distinctly reveals the private parts of your body and attracts attention to those parts. Regarding such clothing, my own husband, a bishop in one of the BYU wards, said: "Girls and guys apparently don't realize what effect this has on the opposite sex. There is no question that immodest clothing encourages immoral thoughts, which so often lead to immoral actions." No wonder our Church leaders have told us not to wear such attire.

Maybe you're thinking about how much this outfit cost you. It wasn't cheap. You may say, "No way am I going to throw away a forty-dollar outfit." Let me try to help you put it into perspective. God is the Father of your spirit, and he is the one who gave you this opportunity to have a body. He loves you more than you could ever comprehend. You are his child. Don't give *him* that stay-out-of-my-life look. He wants you to have the greatest joy possible . . . remember? Everything he reveals to the prophet and inspires you to do will lead you to that happiness. You can't argue with that kind of love. Forty dollars is nothing compared to a chance to return that love and obey him.

One young mother I know shared an experience she had when she was a teenager. An understanding that she was a daughter of God and the knowledge that she enjoyed a "noble birthright" were important principles in her personal value system. She said that as a young person she had tried very hard to live the teachings of the gospel and had generally felt she was doing a pretty good job of it. She told me about attending a spiritually enriching youth conference and then said: "I began examining my life to see what I needed to change. I knew I lived the law of chastity, observed the Word of Wisdom, was an honest person, and was trying to improve in other areas of my life. The only thing I really questioned was my swimsuit. It wasn't as modest as it should have been. I liked it, but I decided wearing it wasn't worth the risk of losing all I'd worked so hard to achieve spiritually. So I threw it away."

Are you a young person who has a testimony and who claims to be true to the Savior but who insists it is okay to wear revealing swimsuits or other immodest clothing? Please take a minute right now and think about your clothes. Both guys and girls. I mean *really examine* them. Put them on and then stand in front of the mirror and ask yourself if your Heavenly Father would approve. If you have any question, please remember the saying so often used by our Church leaders: "If in doubt, don't do it." Have the courage to get rid of anything in your life, including clothing, that doesn't accurately reflect what you are trying to be and that isn't in harmony with Church teachings.

That reminds me of a time when my daughter came home

after school and discovered a box of hand-me-down clothes some friends had sent us. The girls in that family were older than my daughter, and they had thoughtfully sent boxes of clothes before. Our daughter loved the designer fashions they would discard because they had grown out of them. This time she saw a swimsuit in the box. She needed a new one. With delight she held up the skimpy piece of fabric and said, "Mom. Look, a swimming suit!" I said, "Where is it?"

Indignantly she retorted, "It's right here, and I like it." I didn't want her to like it. There were things about it that just weren't modest. But I didn't want to be the bad guy who says, "No! You can't have it!" I hate saying no to my kids. I know, you think parents stay up nights just thinking of ways to say no. Well, we don't. It's much more fun to say yes, because you seem to like us so much more when we do.

Just then I had an ingenious idea, so good it had to have come from the Holy Ghost. I knew what to tell my daughter, and it wasn't no.

"Honey," I said, "this modesty business is not my idea. I go along with it, but it's not my idea." Then, pointing upward, I said, "It's his. Heavenly Father's the one who told the prophet to tell us to be modest. Not me. So if you have a problem with that, maybe you should talk it over with him." Then I suggested she go to her room, shut the door, put on the swimming suit, and kneel down and ask Heavenly Father if it was okay to wear.

With slightly more arrogance and confidence than usual, she said, "I'll do it!"

As soon as her door shut I began to pray. Oh, how I wanted her to make a right choice. Ten minutes later she came out, tossed the swimsuit to me and, somewhat humbled, said, "Give it to Deseret Industries."

I don't know what happened in her room, but whatever it was she came away knowing that she shouldn't wear that suit.

Do you know you can do that? If you have any question about a certain teaching of the Church, you too can kneel down and ask your Heavenly Father what's right for you. Pay attention to how you feel, because he generally answers through your feelings. You may have a feeling of peace, sometimes even a strong, burning feeling, if it's right. Or, you may be left with a "stupor of thought" as mentioned in Section 9 of the Doctrine and Covenants. That feeling of uncertainty is a signal — "If in doubt, don't do it."

A multitude of young men in the Church would be relieved if all the young women in the Church would take greater care to dress modestly. I was speaking about modesty at an informal fireside recently when a group of young men started to laugh. I asked, "Want to share what's funny?" One of the young men consented. "Girls just don't get it," he said. "A girl came into church this morning wearing a low-cut dress. Well . . . she stooped over to pick up something, and you wouldn't believe the show we got!" They all laughed again. "We've been laughing ever since." Then he got serious. "How are we supposed to keep our minds on the sacrament with that kind of show going on?"

I don't condone laughing at girls, but neither do I condone dressing in a way that invites laughter or in a way that drives the Spirit away. We all have a responsibility, not only to ourselves but to others, to invite the Spirit, not drive it away.

That reminds me of an experience I had several years ago. It was the late sixties, the first miniskirt era, and I had a calling to work with the young women. A seventeen-year-old young man who was not LDS had come to live with us for a time. He was a fine young man, and we hoped to be able to share the gospel with him. A few days after he moved in, he came home from school somewhat discouraged. I asked him what was wrong and was surprised when he replied, "I don't think there's a virgin left in the world." He had lost all confidence in the girls he associated with at school.

I thought this was the perfect chance to introduce him to the gospel. I said, "I know where there's a whole church full of them." His curiosity was aroused. I told him about MIA, which was scheduled to be held that very night, and invited him to come. The invitation was too good to refuse, and he accepted.

He stood in the foyer of the meetinghouse, watching the girls as they came through the door. We leaders had been working with these girls, trying very hard to persuade them to dress modestly, but most of them were caught up in the latest styles, and many came to MIA wearing their short skirts.

On the way home after the meeting, he said, "I thought you said these girls were virgins." I immediately responded, "They are! I know these girls, and I feel confident to say they live the law of chastity."

He looked right at me and asked, "Then why don't they dress like it?"

Wow, what a lesson for these young women! More and more I am discovering why the apostle Paul said, "Abstain from all appearance of evil" (1 Thessalonians 5:22).

When one of my returned-missionary nephews was visiting me one day, I asked him about a girl he had been dating. He said, "Oh, we're not dating any more." Though they hadn't dated long, I had the impression he had been quite interested in her. She had seemed to be a good LDS girl. I asked what happened.

"I was starting to fall for her," he said, "and . . . well. . . to tell you the truth, she started wearing clothes that were a little too revealing. I don't mean to sound stuffy, but, honestly, I began to feel uncomfortable. Not because she wasn't pretty to look at, but because I didn't like what it made me think about. I've been trying all my life to be morally clean, and . . . well, I just couldn't chance it, so I broke it off." A few years later he dated and eventually married a lovely young woman who knew how to dress fashionably and modestly. It was a beautiful temple wedding that both had lived worthy to have.

In addition to dressing modestly ourselves, we ought to take care not to encourage immodest dress in others. What kind of message does it send when young men whistle and make catcalls at girls in revealing clothing? An insecure girl may be confused and decide to wear inappropriate clothing just to attract attention. Wise up, young men. Don't let your response be as irresponsible as her poor choice of clothing.

Young women also need to be aware of how ridiculous they appear when they wear revealing outfits. While they may not be able to ignore an immodestly dressed woman, young men are generally embarrassed by such displays. A young woman who wears immodest clothing also runs the risk of being misjudged and labeled as something she doesn't intend. And revealing clothing promotes lascivious thoughts that can ultimately lead to immorality. Young men and young women both need to stop playing on the enemy's team. It's too risky.

Something that happened in 1985 reflected favorably on the stand the Church takes on modesty. Danny Ainge and Greg Kite, former BYU basketball players, both ended up playing for the Boston Celtics in the NBA. As a birthday prank in "honor" of Bill Walton's thirty-third birthday, someone hired a female stripper to disrobe in front of the big center and his teammates. A newspaper report noted: "Mormon pro basketball players Danny Ainge and Greg Kite may not be burning up the court with their play but they came through the other day when it counted. . . . Teammates Ainge and Kite, both Mormons, refused to watch" (*Latter-Day Sentinel,* 14 Dec. 1985, p. 4).

I firmly believe that how we respond to the immodesty of others has everything to do with how we value our own modesty. We cannot be double-minded. We are either for the Lord or against him on this issue. There is no middle ground. I do not believe we can look upon another's immodesty, find pleasure in it — even encourage it with complimentary responses — and be in the Lord's good graces. If he says it's not appropriate and if we are on the Lord's side, we must respond as Greg and Danny did and refuse to watch.

At times some young men and young women may unwittingly behave immodestly. For instance, a young woman may be wearing a modest skirt or pants, but if she sits carelessly, with her legs apart, those sitting across from her may get quite a view. That is embarrassing for her and for those who may observe her. Care enough about yourself to be aware of how you're sitting or bending and of what your posture may reveal or suggest. One professional counselor has observed, "Immodest positioning of the body can easily be taken as a signal that says, 'My body's available.' "

Attention you might draw to yourself by dressing immodestly is temporary and shallow. On the other hand, there's something wonderful about the way people respond to you when you dress and behave modestly. People are then free to focus on the real you — your fun personality, your smile, your conversation, your testimony, and all the other elements that make you interesting, unique, and beautiful. Wouldn't you rather be noticed for such reasons instead of for a willingness to expose your body inappropriately?

I remember one afternoon when I was walking along a beach in California, feeling dismayed at the lack of modesty. Then I noticed a group of young people playing volleyball. In the midst of several boys on one team was a pretty girl who was modestly dressed in tee shirt and shorts. She was laughing and having a great time, as were the boys on her team. She was obviously self-confident and popular. (I could tell the boys liked her by the way they responded to her.) Her modest outfit didn't put her at any disadvantage I could see. In fact, the more scantily clad girls on the beach were not enjoying anywhere near the attention this girl was getting.

One bishop told me that he had been working with a young woman who had morally transgressed and who was trying with all her heart and might to repent. He was impressed with her sincere desire to make her repentance complete. He said he had observed, before her confession, that her clothes were not always as modest as they should have been. Without mentioning that to her, he met and prayed with her regularly, helping her find ways to strengthen her testimony of the Savior. He said, "I watched her, and as her testimony grew, something interesting happened to her wardrobe. The stronger she became spiritually, the more modest her wardrobe became." His observation was a witness that those who seek the Spirit regard their bodies as sacred and dress in harmony with that Spirit.

As I observe the fashions of the day, I realize that you don't live in the era of the strapless evening gown, as I did. Instead, you live in the era of the gownless evening strap. But you'll make it. I know you can, because President Ezra

Taft Benson said: "It is not by chance that you have been reserved to come to earth in this last dispensation of the fulness of times. . . . You are 'youth of the noble birthright' " ("To the Young Women of the Church," *Ensign,* Nov. 1986, p. 81).

With all my heart I hope you will remember who you are and why you came to earth. I pray that you will prove to your Heavenly Father how much you love him by actions that are in harmony with his teachings. Remember, he loves you. He loves you so much he even gave his Only Begotten Son, Jesus Christ, to sacrifice all, just for you. One way you can show your gratitude and love for him is to honor the body he has given you by dressing and behaving modestly. Remember, though fashions may change, modesty is always in style.

CHAPTER 5

THE CONSEQUENCES OF SEXUAL SIN

RANDAL A. WRIGHT

One day while I was sitting at my desk at the LDS institute where I served as director, a former student named Veronica suddenly burst into my office. She was literally jumping up and down with excitement. I couldn't imagine what all the commotion was about. I thought maybe she had won the Publisher's Clearing House million-dollar prize or something. When she finally calmed down enough to speak, she blurted out her news. "I'm pregnant!" she exclaimed. Her excitement was greater than that of most newly expectant mothers because for many years doctors had doubted her ability even to conceive. And now she was pregnant. All of us who knew her were ecstatic over this news.

What a contrast this visit was to another I received. The institute secretary knocked on my door and said a young woman wanted to talk to me. I could tell something was seriously wrong as soon as Maria walked through the door. Concern was written all over her face. When I asked how she was doing, she burst into tears. I had no idea what was wrong and had to wait until she got control of her emotions to find out. At first I thought maybe a loved one had died or that she had some incurable disease. It wasn't either of these things. When she finally managed to compose herself, she announced somberly, "I'm pregnant."

Isn't that interesting? Maria uttered the very same words Veronica had spoken. But there was a marked contrast in the countenances of these two young women and a huge difference in how they viewed their conditions. What do you think made the difference?

The difference lay in the timing and the circumstances of the two pregnancies. Veronica had been married in the temple to a worthy returned missionary. The couple was active in the Church and trying to live the Lord's commandments. They viewed having a child as a blessing. Maria, on the other hand, had decided it was not important to wait for marriage to share sexual intimacies with a young man. She was devastated when, after she informed him of her pregnancy, he said he wanted nothing more to do with her. So, while Veronica's news was greeted with joy and happiness by all who loved her, Maria's news brought regret, shame, sorrow, and misery to her and disappointment to her loved ones.

Between tearful interludes, Maria asked me a compelling question: "Is there an easy way out of this?"

Put yourself in my place. How would *you* have answered that question? I was unable to think of an easy way out of her problem. I could only wish with her that she had never gotten herself into the situation in the first place. Maria was learning a hard lesson — that there is always a terrible price to pay for disobedience.

President Ezra Taft Benson has said: "The plaguing sin of this generation is sexual immorality. . . . It permeates our society" ("Cleansing the Inner Vessel," *Ensign,* May 1986, p. 4). As I travel around the Church, the concern I hear most often expressed by priesthood leaders and parents about their youth is that of immorality. It is a matter of great concern to President Benson also. He has declared: "Sexual immorality is a viper that is striking not only in the world, but in the Church today. Not to admit it is to be dangerously complacent or is like putting one's head in the sand" (*God, Family, Country: Our Three Great Loyalties* [Salt Lake City: Deseret Book Co., 1974], p. 239).

A friend of mine asked approximately 250 LDS students the following question on an anonymous questionnaire: "If you could commit one 'free sin' with no consequences, which sin would you choose?" More than 80 percent of the students said that they would use their "free sin" to break the law of chastity.

Another teacher asked a group of LDS seminary students to rank a long list of sins. The results were alarming. In order of seriousness, these students ranked breaking the Word of Wisdom first and breaking the law of chastity fifth. As I read the results of this survey, the words of Elder Ezra Taft Benson came to mind: "So garbled in values have our morals become that some youth would not dare touch a cigaret but freely engage in petting. Both are wrong, but one is infinitely more serious than the other" ("Three Threatening Dangers," *Improvement Era,* Dec. 1964, p. 1069). How do you rank breaking the law of chastity?

How did the sin that is described in the scriptures as the "most abominable above all sins save it be the shedding of innocent blood or denying the Holy Ghost" (Alma 39:5) become so commonplace and accepted in our society? How did we get to the point where some, even in the Church, fail to realize the seriousness of sexual sin? We know that Satan loves to see people fall. I think he has a lot to do with this attitude in our society today.

Satan is very clever. After thousands of years of experience, he knows just how to deceive. He knows when and where to strike his victims. He will try everything in his power to keep youth from reaching their divine potential. Commenting on Satan's tactics, President Spencer W. Kimball declared: "He will use his logic to confuse and his rationalizations to destroy. He will shade meanings, open doors an inch at a time, and lead from purest white through all the shades of gray to the darkest black" ("President Kimball Speaks Out on Morality," *Ensign,* Nov. 1980, p. 94).

Satan is well aware of the strong sexual drive that Heavenly Father has placed within His children. That divinely implanted instinct ensures the perpetuation of the human race, and intimate expressions of affection fill basic needs in all of us. It suits Satan's purposes if he can persuade us to misuse the sacred powers of procreation or to express the intimacies of marriage before it is time. Immoral behavior diverts us from the gospel path, deprives us of the Spirit, and often leaves emotional scars that are carried into adulthood. Many youth have succumbed to this kind of temptation and experienced the sorrow that results.

Before we can consider possible solutions to the "plaguing sin," we need to look more closely at the consequences of immoral behavior. It is not pleasant, but it is necessary if we are to fully understand what we're up against.

CHANGES IN ATTITUDE TOWARD SEXUAL MATTERS

Sexual attitudes and behavior have changed dramatically since your grandparents, and even your parents, were teenagers. Premarital sex was less common then and was viewed as morally and socially wrong. From the late 1960s to the present, however, society has adopted a much more liberal attitude toward sexual matters. Today's youth have grown up in a permissive environment and have developed a viewpoint that is often vastly different from that of their parents or grandparents. Many young people are yielding to the idea that there is no need to "wait until marriage." A rapid rise in the proportion of youth who are engaging in heavy petting and premarital sex has alarmed Church leaders and parents.

The sexual revolution seems to have moved from the college campus down to the high school and now is moving into our junior high schools. A 1989 national study revealed that 33 percent of all boys had experienced sex by age fifteen (the year before they should even date). By age sixteen, 50 percent had engaged in sex, and by age nineteen (the age when LDS young men should go on missions), 86 percent of the young men surveyed had had sexual relations (*Newsweek,* June 1990, p. 27).

Why are so many falling into this sin when the reward is so meager and the consequences so horrendous? Can you think of any *good* reason to engage in sexual relations outside the marriage covenant? Can anything of value be gained from this behavior? What are the consequences? Dr. Henry A. Bowman made this thought-provoking statement: "When all is said and done, there is nothing gained from pre-marital adventure except immediate pleasure and that at tremendous risk and exorbitant cost. No really intelligent person will burn a cathedral to fry an egg, even to satisfy a *ravenous* appetite" (quoted by Hugh B. Brown, in *Purity Is Power* [Salt Lake City: The Church of Jesus Christ of Latter-day Saints, 1978], p. 24).

Satan depends for his success on humanity's willingness to disregard long-term consequences in order to satisfy immediate appetites. His work prospers because momentary pleasure appeals to huge numbers of people. Here are two simple formulas that illustrate the difference between the forces that are battling for the minds of men:

Satan = immediate gratification with long-term agony and grief as the "reward."

Jesus Christ = short-term self-discipline with long-term joy and happiness as the reward.

Because the agony and grief that result when we follow Satan is often somewhat delayed, many fail to realize they have been trapped until it is too late.

A young man who is a member of the Church recently told me that he had committed a "serious sin" with his nonmember girlfriend. He said that after the experience, he became physically ill because of the tremendous guilt that overcame him. His comment to me was unforgettable. He said, "All my life I've heard that we shouldn't have premarital sex because it is wrong. But I have also been told that if we make mistakes, we can repent and be forgiven. Repentance sounded so simple and easy." And then came his haunting question, "Why didn't anyone ever tell me about the consequences of sin and the feeling of nausea I would have afterward?" Of course, our prophets have taught this lesson repeatedly, but many youth fail to listen.

Since that experience, I have thought deeply about the consequences of sexual sin and have begun to compile a list of dreadful results. Please realize that this is only a partial list and in no way represents all the dangers. As you think about what you have observed, you will probably think of other things that could be added to the list.

CONSEQUENCES OF SEXUAL SIN

Personal Peace and Happiness Are Destroyed

Our Heavenly Father has blessed each of us with a conscience or the Light of Christ. We are born with it, and it works something like an alarm. When we walk too close to the line that separates right from wrong, this special warning signal alerts us that we are stepping into dangerous territory. When we break a commandment, the alarm's clamor can be so loud and insistent it can be emotionally agonizing. On the other hand, when we keep the commandments, our conscience remains quiet.

Those involved in sexual sin often suffer from depression, anxiety, guilt, worry, low self-esteem, and remorse. Is it a coincidence that teen suicide rates have increased at almost the same rate as teen sexual activity has increased? A recent study of young adolescents found that "girls who'd had sex were six times more likely to attempt suicide" than those who were still virgins (*USA Today*, 6 Feb. 1991, Sec. D, p. 1).

The world speaks of getting "protection" for illicit sex. But there is no protection from the unhappiness and guilt associated with this sin. A lifetime of self-discipline and happiness can be ruined in a matter of minutes. Even though the Lord can restore spiritual virtue by deep repentance, there will be only one "first time" physically. Virginity is something that can be given only once; it can never be recovered if it is surrendered. This first experience remains forever embedded in a person's memory.

How much better to be able to remember the "first time" as a sacred act of love made legitimate by marriage in the holy temple, rather than to recall it as a shameful act of lust. Physical love might be compared to money kept in a savings account. Likewise, we might accumulate and safeguard our desires until they can be given to an eternal mate as a wedding present. Imagine the joy and the powerful emotional bonding that would accompany the presentation of such a gift. There is only one path to happiness, and that is through virtuous living.

Reputations Are Damaged

Have you ever heard a rumor that someone you know has broken the law of chastity? The secret always seems to get out. Satan whispers to his victim that "no one will know" about the deed. Partners in sin hope that the other will not tell what happened. Such secrets are rarely kept. Guilt may persuade a young woman to confide in a friend. All too often a young man will brag of his conquest to his buddies. Word soon spreads, and a young woman unknowingly becomes the talk of the locker room. In the end, devastated young men and young women are left with severely damaged reputations.

Rumors spread quickly not only to peers but to adults as well. Bishops, youth advisers, and even parents often find out about the deed from concerned friends within a short time.

We must remember that even if no one on earth is aware of the sin, someone is always watching. Jesus Christ said, "Hearken, O ye people of my church, saith the voice of him who dwells on high, and whose *eyes are upon all men*" (D&C 1:1; emphasis added).

Those who are tempted to break the moral code should remember the words of Henry Wheeler Shaw: "A broken reputation is like a broken vase—it may be mended, but it always shows where the break was!" (*International Dictionary of Thoughts* [Chicago: J.G. Ferguson Publishing Co., 1969], p. 625). Though it is possible for the transgressor to repent and change his or her behavior and though the Lord can and will forgive, society always seems reluctant to forget what it learns of this sort of behavior.

Trust in Future Relationships Is Threatened

Trust is the foundation of healthy relationships, particularly the marriage relationship. If marriage partners have been sexually active with others before their marriage, that frequently introduces feelings of insecurity and jealousy. There may be lingering suspicion based on the knowledge that their mate has had previous problems controlling his or her physical desires. Couples who may have otherwise been virtuous but who surrendered to temptation during their courtship and engagement are often troubled by the memory of their immoral behavior. Such memories may well plague their legitimate sexual relationship, robbing them of the joy and happiness that should be present. Premarital sexual experience is often a destructive force that subtly erodes the trust that is so vital in a marriage relationship. One prominent LDS marriage counselor observed that a vast majority of those he sees for counseling have been involved in premarital sex to some degree. These considerations may have been what President David O. McKay had in mind when he said, "He who is unchaste in young manhood is untrue to a trust given to him by the parents of the girl, and she who is unchaste in maidenhood is untrue to her future husband, and lays the foundation of unhappiness in the home, suspicion, and discord" (*Stepping Stones to an Abundant Life* [Salt Lake City: Deseret Book Co., 1971], p. 11).

Sexual activity is often a crutch that keeps a premarital relationship together. Contrary to what might be supposed, a sexual relationship does not help an unmarried couple bond in meaningful ways, and sex often becomes a destructive thing. Instead of getting to know each other and finding out if they really are in love, many couples neglect to explore other facets of their relationship and spend their time together giving vent to their passions. With their feelings for each other founded on lust instead of love, many couples marry, only to discover that they are otherwise incompatible. This discovery is particularly harmful if communication skills have not been cultivated. Then the physical alliance begins to dominate. It has been shown that a marriage based mostly on a sexual relationship—where the couple has not bonded spiritually, intellectually, and emotionally—is not likely to endure the stresses life puts on any couple. A virtuous couple is free to build a relationship on trust that can endure the trials of marriage.

Sexually Transmitted Diseases May Be Passed Along

One serious consequence of premarital sex is the danger of getting sexually transmitted diseases. These frightening diseases now exist in epidemic profusion. James Mason gives these alarming figures: "There are twenty-three identified sexually transmitted diseases with 10 million new cases diagnosed annually—two-thirds among young adults" (*Church News*, 24 Oct. 1988, p. 6).

Medical authorities say that a single sexual encounter can infect a person with as many as five different sexually transmitted diseases. When a person is casual about sexual relations, he or she takes the chance that the partner has also been casual. All of these diseases are frightful, but the introduction of AIDS into the world makes the practice of casual sex one of the most dangerous games imaginable. Medical experts say that the only people who are not at risk of these diseases are those who are monogamous for life with a partner who is also monogamous. That means having only one partner who also has only one partner. No wonder the Lord said, "Thou shalt love thy wife with all thy heart, and shalt cleave unto her and *none else"* (D&C 42:22; emphasis added).

Pregnancy May Result

Another huge tragedy of premarital sex is illegitimate pregnancy. Infants come from the Lord's presence pure, innocent, vulnerable, and entirely dependent. Clearly, each baby deserves to be born into a safe environment where he or she can be loved, nurtured, and trained. That is best accomplished when the parents are mature, married to each other, and capable of acting responsibly. By trifling with the sacred powers we possess to procreate life, we violate God's plan and offend him by putting one of his precious ones in jeopardy.

When an unmarried young woman becomes pregnant, she and her partner immediately surrender their freedom and are confronted with essentially five choices:

1. *Marriage.* This option is becoming less frequently chosen with each passing year. When forced marriages do occur, they are usually between couples who may not have otherwise married. That may help explain why the United States has the highest divorce rate in the world. One study shows that 85 percent of unwed fathers will eventually abandon the woman who bears their child. That means that only 15 percent of young fathers actually marry their pregnant girlfriend and stay married.

2. *Abortion.* When asked recently what they thought the best solution to a teen pregnancy was, more than 50 percent

of the high school students who were surveyed said having an abortion was the best decision. Abortion is condemned by our Church leaders as a great evil and a serious transgression. Millions of young men and women in the world are suffering the guilt and anguish of having taken the life of their own child. It is impossible to calculate the extent of their remorse. But large numbers of those who have been a party to abortion report having flashbacks, nightmares, and a preoccupation with the aborted child—even years after the occurrence.

3. *Cohabitation.* Living together as husband and wife without legal or religious sanction is a gross sin, but the practice is dramatically increasing in the United States and throughout the world. Between 1960 and 1988 the estimated number of unmarried couples living together in the United States rose from 439,000 to 2.6 million (U.S. Census Bureau).

4. *Adoption.* This option is often recommended to those who do not have the opportunity or choose not to marry. The lives of many married but childless couples have been blessed by being able to adopt children born to unwed mothers; however, teenaged girls rarely choose this option (95 percent now keep their babies, even though thousands of childless couples are waiting to adopt).

5. *Single parenthood.* The United States now has the highest birthrate to teenaged parents in the Western world. Out-of-wedlock births among adolescents have increased dramatically over the past four decades. Adolescent pregnancy is given as the major cause for girls dropping out of school.

When a young single mother chooses to raise her baby alone, she often experiences some harsh realities. Dating becomes difficult because of the amount of time and attention demanded by her infant and by the stigma the unwed mother often has to bear. Isolation from friends may also result. Think for a moment about being saddled with financial responsibilities, the loss of social relationships, and the drudgery of caring for a child. After a young woman bears a child, there is usually no more hanging out with friends, planning sleep-overs, going out to eat, buying lots of clothes, or having money for recreation.

Sexual Activity May Become Addictive

Like all vices, premarital sexual behavior can be addictive and lead an unsuspecting young person into bondage. Research shows that teens who have had sexual relations seldom stop with one experience. Often their craving for intimacy becomes an obsession, dominating relationships and turning its desperate participants into slaves of sensuality. Like skiing down a steep mountain, the process is much easier to begin than to stop. When sexual opportunities are denied after being fulfilled in the past, lust often finds temporary relief in other immoral ways, such as indulgence in pornography. That may help explain the increase in other sexual perversions in our society.

Resistance to Other Sins Is Weakened

Another dangerous side effect of sexual sin is that it destroys hope and often leads to other sins. A common feeling among those involved is, "I have already messed up, so why even try?" The adversary must love this defeatist attitude. Young people who are discouraged and hopeless often lower their defenses and, as though a protective wall has come down, allow other sins to rush in.

Researchers have found that sexually experienced girls are five times more likely to be suspended from school than those who have never had sex, and they are ten times more likely to have used marijuana. Boys with sexual experience are six times more likely to have used alcohol, five times more likely to have used marijuana, and ten times more likely to have been in a car with a drug-using driver (*USA Today*, 6 Feb. 1991, Sec. D, p. 1).

Elder Hugh B. Brown was correct when he said, "One of the most lethal weapons used by Lucifer against the first offender is the disarming implication that, having once sinned, there is no hope and that therefore he might just as well surrender and sample all the other 'scented poisons' prepared for his complete destruction" (*Purity Is Power*, p. 31).

The Lord's Spirit Is Lost

Without the guidance and protection of the Spirit of the Lord, we struggle less effectively to overcome temptations. Immorality shatters a person's relationship with the Spirit. President Benson confirmed that when he said: "No sin is causing the loss of the Spirit of the Lord among our people more today than sexual promiscuity. It is causing our people to stumble, damning their growth, darkening their spiritual powers, and making them subject to other sins" (*God, Family, Country*, pp. 239–40).

Spiritual progress is blocked by immorality. Everything that is really important in life is put on hold unless individuals who have behaved immorally properly repent. "But whoso committeth adultery with a woman lacketh understanding: he that doeth it destroyeth his own soul" (Proverbs 6:32).

Those involved in sexual immorality often lose the desire to pray, to read the scriptures, to share the gospel, or to give compassionate service. They often feel uncomfortable around their parents or their bishop, advisers, and other Church members. Avoiding these contacts, most find it difficult to maintain their activity in the Church, "for every one that doeth evil hateth the light, neither cometh to the light, lest his deeds should be reproved" (John 3:20). Immoral people find themselves feeling terribly alone and abandoned. Most youth who have committed grievous sins struggle even to like themselves.

WHAT CAN YOU DO?

A great deal more could be said about immorality—how it destroys families and nations. But we are not talking about nations. We are talking about what can be done about temptations you may have experienced. How does all this apply in your life, in your relationships, and in the things you are struggling with?

Perhaps you have allowed yourself to fantasize about sexual matters or find yourself in a relationship where you are being pressured to behave in ways you know are not right. Maybe what you have read in books or magazines has confused you—there are many ignorant or evil people in the world who promote premarital sex, petting, and passionate behavior in dating. These things are all glorified in the movies and on television.

Friends who are not clear on this subject will often argue persuasively that it is natural and even healthy to give expression to sexuality before marriage. A young person who is trying to live the commandments can easily become confused by the conflicting voices.

If you are confused on this issue or if you have not made up your mind and are reading this hoping to find some answers or the strength to resist temptation, *you can be certain that having sex before marriage is wrong.* Doing so is a sin, and it complicates life, results in unhappiness, puts the probability of missionary service and temple marriage in doubt, puts people at risk for disease and pregnancy, and *always* drives away the Spirit of the Lord.

If you have yielded to temptation and broken the law of chastity, please read chapter 13 in this book. Be assured there is still hope.

But what can you do if you are struggling and are in a situation where pressure is being put upon you? Consider the warnings listed above. Talk about your confusion with your parents, bishop, adviser, or seminary or institute teacher. Pray for strength. Ask for a blessing. Read the scriptures. Avoid suggestive or sexually provocative movies, music, and literature, and get out of dangerous relationships.

Bear in mind the reward for being virtuous. Imagine how you will feel if you are able to sit in your interviews with your bishop or stake president and honestly declare your worthiness to go on a mission or to receive a temple recommend. Think how it will be to take your sweetheart's hand and one day walk into the temple, feeling fresh, clean, virtuous, and worthy in every way to be there. Set a goal to offer yourself as a clean and worthy companion to your marriage partner.

Our Heavenly Father doesn't want us to be forced to make agonizing decisions about out-of-wedlock pregnancies, sexually transmitted diseases, damaged reputations, and addictions, so he has given us a solution—a solution so simple that its obviousness seems to have eluded the supposedly great minds of our society. The answer is abstinence from sexual activity before marriage and fidelity after marriage.

THE SIN OF FORNICATION

VIKKI D. MARSHALL

She lingered after class until all the others had filed out and then slowly approached my desk. Her whole body warned me that something was troubling her. She had difficulty looking at me. Her head was bowed and her voice subdued. And she looked extremely nervous.

"Sister Marshall, could I speak with you?"

I closed the door to the classroom, anticipating something serious, although I could not have guessed what it might be. This intelligent and energetic seventeen-year-old beauty had never been anything but a delight to have in seminary. She was full of life and promise, and with her senior year nearly behind her, she appeared to enjoy the prospect of a brilliant future.

"Sister Marshall," she said quietly, "this will be my last day in seminary."

Her statement caught me completely by surprise. It was late April and the senior students were already planning graduation activities. Could she and her family be moving? Was this the reason she looked so sad? And then she said the one thing I would never have supposed I would hear from this four-year, straight-A, seminary student.

"I'm pregnant, Sister Marshall."

Royal Generation. Noble and Great Ones. These are just a few of the terms used to characterize Mormon youth of today. I know that many of you are weary of being reminded of everything those titles suggest. I've heard many of my seminary students complain, "We're tired of being called 'Saturday's Warriors'! It's too much responsibility! Couldn't we have just one weekend off to do what we want, without having to feel the guilt on Sunday morning?"

You may not be comfortable being singled out for this kind of responsibility, but that's the way it is. For many reasons, some of which we may not know, your turn on earth is now—during the time when the earth and its inhabitants are being prepared for the second coming of the Savior. You have the opportunity to play a key role both in the world and in the Church.

You are also living at a time when sinful behavior is increasing in the world. Satan has taken hold of the hearts of many. There is a great deal of evidence that humans are increasingly indifferent to God or defiant of his commandments. Moreover, spokesmen for evil are persuasive, and it is not always easy to tell what is right and what is wrong or who is telling the truth and who is not. This is the world into which you were born. Your challenge is to overcome the evil that surrounds you and keep the commandments. By doing so, you will "prove yourself" and qualify to return to Heavenly Father's presence.

One of the greatest temptations you will confront during your lifetime is the temptation to misuse your sexual powers. I hope you will accept my counsel on this important subject.

Heavenly Father, your parents, and your Church teachers and leaders understand what your mission is, but they are not the only ones. Satan knows, and he will try everything in his power to stop you, much in the same way he desperately tried to stop our Lord from carrying out his atoning sacrifice. After Jesus had fasted and prayed in the wilderness for forty days, Satan came, tempting him with food, with wealth, and with worldly power—appealing in each case to his mortal passions (see Luke 4). Fortunately for us, Christ was able to resist the temptations. By doing so he further prepared himself for his mission and provided us with a powerful example.

Satan tempts us to be disobedient in a similar way—by appealing to *our* passions. It suits his purposes if he can somehow get us to surrender control of our sexual appetites. The great danger to young people in this regard is sexual immorality and, specifically, the sin of fornication.

Fornication is defined by a latter-day apostle as "illicit sexual intercourse on the part of an unmarried person" (Bruce R. McConkie, *Mormon Doctrine*, 2d ed. [Salt Lake City: Bookcraft, 1966], p. 298). To be more specific, if you are unmarried and you "go to bed with," "sleep with," or "make love to" someone, you are guilty of committing fornication. Moreover, it is not a minor transgression but rather one of the most serious sins, "ranking close to adultery in wickedness," according to Elder McConkie. It is a sin that results in serious consequences.

One of the things that is so scary about growing up at this time is that so many people in the world—including young people—do not seem to understand how wrong it is to commit fornication. Too many young people engage in sex recreationally, as though it were an acceptable dating activity.

Trifling with the sacred powers of reproduction grossly offends our Father in Heaven. President Joseph F. Smith explained: "Sexual union is lawful in wedlock, and if participated in with right intent is honorable and sanctifying. But without the bonds of marriage, sexual indulgence is a debasing sin, abominable in the sight of Deity" (*Gospel Doctrine* [Salt Lake City: Deseret Book Co., 1939], p. 309). Among other reasons, the sin of fornication offends Heavenly Father because of the suffering it caused Jesus in the Garden of Gethsemane and on the cross. When you are tempted, you might reflect on how he bled from every pore of his precious body (see D&C 19:15–19). In light of that suffering, is it any wonder that our Heavenly Father is offended when his children so carelessly violate this or any other commandment?

You may be wondering what makes fornication sinful. Is the sin in the act of sexual intercourse itself? Certainly not! Intercourse is a sacred act, ordained by God to allow us, his children, to be cocreators with him. When sanctified by marriage, it is a beautiful expression of love and serves to bind the man and woman together, physically, emotionally, and spiritually. Within the bonds of marriage, it is to be enjoyed.

Could the sin lie in the fact that teens and young adults are simply too young to really know what love is? Is it the emotional immaturity of the participants that makes fornication sinful? No. When most members of the older generation think back, they remember that they were never more romantically in love than when they were young. Teen love is a real and tangible thing and is as true an emotion as any you will ever feel. I have all the respect in the world for your emotions. If you tell me, "Sister Marshall, you don't understand. It's different with us. We're in love!" I would never insult you by dismissing your feelings as trivial. The only difference between the love you feel and the love your parents share is that your love hasn't had the time to fully mature. And that is not your fault. You simply have not lived long enough yet. No, your youthful emotions are not what makes fornication sinful.

Could the sin be in the potential for pregnancy? Well, pregnancy outside marriage is certainly something to consider. Becoming pregnant if you are married is one of the great blessings of life. Bringing children into the world is an essential part of the plan of salvation. There is no sin in a newborn baby, regardless of the conditions of its birth. Clothed in their precious little bodies, these spirits come into this world fresh from the presence of the Father. But if we bring an infant into this world outside the bonds of marriage, we put the little one at risk, and we violate the plan the Lord instituted for the birth of children.

May I submit that the sin of fornication, besides being a direct violation of a commandment, lies in the timing. In other words, *when* you choose to perform that act. If you have sexual relations *before* being legally married, you have, in fact, sinned. If, however, you have sexual relations *after* holy, legal, and binding vows are taken, then you have the Lord's blessing to go ahead. It is a matter of timing and obedience.

I took her in my arms and held her there as she and I cried together. Her tears were of remorse and fear of the unknown, mine of anger at Satan for beguiling another of Heavenly Father's choicest children. I thought of how difficult it must have been for her to tell me, her seminary teacher. How much more difficult it must have been when she told her parents and watched as the light left their eyes. And if it was hard for her to tell me and her parents, how much more difficult it must have been for her to confront the father of her baby, a former boyfriend who had graduated from high school the year before and who was trying to get his act together to go on a mission. "Well, unpack your

bags, elder. You aren't going anywhere. You have new respon-
sibilities." They will have difficult decisions to make. Will they
marry? Will she keep her baby or put it up for adoption? Where
will they live? How shall they support themselves? The list seems
endless. Not exactly the joyful temple marriage she had always
dreamed of.

I have often said there is nothing that anyone can tell your "enlightened generation" about the physical mechanics of lovemaking, that is, how to perform the act. In fact, I used to believe there were a few things your generation could tell ours. But I have changed my mind. As I look around and see how many "babies are having babies," I realize that you may know "how to do it," but you do not necessarily know "how it is done." You need more information. Just because you know how to drive a car and can get from point A to point B, it does not automatically follow that you know how the engine works.

Here is where I will go out on a limb and suggest that by the time you are old enough to read this book, you are ready to know "how it is done." So, where do you go to find out? Certainly not to the "locker room." The information that comes out of there has long since proven itself to be unreliable.

Your first, best source for this information is—are you ready for this?—your parents. Yes, I said, your parents. Right away you are probably thinking, "My parents! Never happen! In your dreams!" My response is, "How do you think you got here?" They do know *something* about this subject.

And Heavenly Father has given them the obligation to teach you about these sacred things in the home. If you have not heard their version, you are cheating yourself. Or, if you think you already know it all, think again. Besides, when mom and dad sit down with you to answer any questions you may have, angels surround them and choirs sing. They may just bring to the topic some wonder, joy, and excitement you will otherwise miss.

Here's something else to consider. Parents bring perspective to their counsel, partly because they have lived longer. Why did the Lord give you to these two "old people" anyway? Why didn't he just send us all down here at the same time, say at the earthly age of seventeen? Picture it. Mom and dad — seventeen; children — seventeen. Seventeen-year-old mom and dad stay home while their seventeen-year-old children go to school. One day the seventeen-year-old daughter comes home with a broken heart, crying to her seventeen-year-old mom. "What should I do?" Mom looks at her and shrugs, "I don't know. I just got here myself!" With age comes experience.

Nevertheless, I am a realist, and I know that some of you cannot — absolutely cannot — discuss this subject with your parents. And, unfortunately, there are some parents who just cannot — absolutely cannot — speak of these things with their children. If that is your situation, then may I suggest that you find some other responsible adult that you can talk to. Now the operative word here is *responsible*. I don't mean someone who graduated from high school last year.

If you are confused about who to ask, then my suggestion would be to go knock on your bishop's door. When he asks you what you need, tell him that you need to know more about how your body works. I will bet you anything, upon hearing that, your bishop will either help you himself or immediately find you a "responsible" adult. The point is, it's time for you to know, and it is important for you to learn it from a responsible source.

What started out as a private act between two people soon became public knowledge. Everyone seemed to know, everyone seemed to be talking about it—in the school yard, in the locker room, and at the family dinner table over mashed potatoes. The young couple had bought into Satan's false assurances: "It's okay. You're in love! Besides, no one will ever know." Like all of his promises, they didn't mean a thing. And once they bought into the sin, Satan left them there to suffer the consequences. What may have seemed so urgent and compelling in the dark while passions were inflamed, left a bitter, ugly aftertaste.

If I may be permitted to make an analogy, Satan promises you a thousand-dollar shopping spree at your favorite clothing store. You can hardly believe it, but it's true. You begin wildly grabbing and trying on all the clothes and accessories you can and handing them to the salesperson. It is so exciting! A dream come true! One outfit after another. You'll be the envy of all your friends. Every time you turn around, Satan is there, encouraging you. Finally, exhausted, you reach the thousand-dollar limit. You wait in anticipation as your selections are bagged to take home. The salesclerk rings up your purchases—one thousand dollars exactly. You turn to Satan, and he hands you a crisp, new, thousand-dollar bill, and you hand it to the salesclerk. There is an uncertain moment as the clerk examines the money and then calls for the manager. Glancing at the bill, he icily informs you that the money is counterfeit. You look around for Satan, but he is nowhere to be found. You feel set-up and desperate. But there is nobody to help you. You face embarrassment and, even worse, possible prosecution.

The manager feels generous and allows you to leave, but you cannot take your new clothes home with you. You leave empty-handed.

It is the same with counterfeit love or lust. It may seem terribly exciting in the initial stages. It may make you feel almost euphoric. But then, when the counterfeit is exposed, you are left alone to face the consequences. You can't take this kind of "love" home with you because it isn't real.

Counterfeit love yields its own fruit, however. Sexually transmitted diseases such as AIDS, syphilis, and herpes abound. Other sins such as masturbation, homosexuality, abortion, prostitution, and rape are a common by-product of lust.

The decision to marry had been made. He felt "obligated," and she had convinced herself that they could "learn" to love each other. He had graduated from high school the year before, and she had also managed to finish school. There was the usual celebration — bridal showers, a civil wedding ceremony performed in the cultural hall of the meetinghouse and, of course, a lavish reception afterwards. For a little time they were caught up in the excitement of it all. They were the envy of their friends. In fact, the celebration of their marriage made some young observers wonder, "Why work so hard to be morally clean if all the worldly rewards are available anyway?"

If you break the commandments and "have to get married," is it really fair or right to expect your parents to help "celebrate the sin" with showers, costly receptions, and the like?

Consider this also. For all the excitement and passion that lead young people into temptation and fornication, there immediately follows a sense of remorse and sadness. That is particularly true if the participants have been taught the gospel and if they have a sense of what the sin represents. Many transgressors describe feeling empty, dirty, ashamed, or angry when the temporary euphoria is over.

I had an experience at Disneyland once that will perhaps illustrate what I am trying to say here.

I love Disneyland. I was there the day it opened in 1955, and I have tried very hard to get back there at least once a year since. My favorite attraction is "Pirates of the Caribbean," a ride I will stand in line an hour and a half for. I never tire of the cool darkness and the magical way we are introduced into the world of the Louisiana Bayou country, complete with fireflies, bullfrogs, and moss hanging from the trees, not to mention Grandpa rocking on his porch with his faithful hound dog by his side. Suddenly we are plunged down two water slides and into the bowels of Disneyland where we are caught up in a pirate fantasy.

Have you noticed that the boats move just fast enough that you cannot really focus too long on any one thing? That's what helps create the illusion. On this particular day, however, there was some mechanical difficulty and the boats stopped. We had to be evacuated, and so the tunnel lights were turned on. The illusion was immediately shattered. Instead of lifelike pirates, I saw only machines, painted with garish, luminescent paint. For all its charm in the darkness, seen in real light, the attraction was revealed to be little more than a carnival illusion.

Those who give away their virtue discover quickly that reality is stark and the aftertaste is bitter. Fornication is a sin without glamor. In fact, giving up your chastity is like trading rubies and pearls for a carnival bauble.

*For the next year or so they both worked hard at regaining
the spirituality they each desperately needed in their lives. They
began attending church together and took care to have their child
blessed. Even though he was able to find a fairly good paying
job, considering he had no degree or work experience, it was still
difficult to make ends meet without her leaving their baby and
seeking work outside the home. But she was willing to do anything
so that they could finally live on their own and not with her
parents or his. It was tough when she occasionally ran into old
classmates who were attending college or preparing for missions
or temple marriages. She envied their carefree lives. It wasn't the
struggle she minded as much as it was the regret she felt in her
heart for all the things that "might have been."*

Earlier, I said that I had all the respect in the world for
your emotions. So does Alma in the Book of Mormon. In
Alma 38:12 he informs us we are to "bridle [our] passions."
Reading that, you might immediately conclude that old Alma
can't relate. Wrong! Notice that Alma doesn't use such words
as *suppress, deny,* or *avoid* your passions. He recognizes they
are real. Rather he picked his word very carefully. We are
to "bridle" our passions. The last time I checked, a bridle
was used for control.

Have you ever had a horse run away with you? If so, then
you can appreciate the function of a bridle. I had such an
experience on a horse named Dollface. (Right away I should
have been suspicious.) Not being a very "horsey" person, I
wasn't real confident as I climbed tentatively into the saddle.
My friend (some friend) handed me the reins and quickly
gave me a few of the basics. Then I was on my own. Holding
the reins loosely, I kicked the horse's sides and said one of
the few words I knew in horse language—"giddyup." I had

no idea it was such a powerful word. Dollface responded to it by breaking into a full gallop across an open field. Being the expert I wasn't, I promptly let go of the reins and took hold of the saddle horn. (Isn't that what it's there for?) Naturally, I now had absolutely no control. I relinquished control of the bridle when I dropped the reins. The horse was able to take me anywhere she wanted, and I was powerless to stop her. Finally, she wore herself out, and after a final jump over a small creek, she stopped. It had been an exciting but scary experience. I sat there with my heart pounding, breathing heavily, and feeling very shaky.

I realized how dangerous the situation had been and how near I had come to being hurt. Moreover, I had not ended up where I had intended to go.

Passions can also run away with you and take you places you don't intend to go. It can be exciting to give them full rein, but it is dangerous.

To help us keep control and steer us away from the brink of disaster, our Church leaders have provided us with some guidelines or standards. These standards are sometimes resented by young people. But the standards are based on the Lord's commandments. And, contrary to what some people think, the commandments are not designed to deprive us of our freedom or to punish us for being young.

Try to imagine a wise and loving Heavenly Father, looking down on us here on earth. From his vantage point he can see all the obstacles and perils in the road ahead. To spare us the sorrow and pain we might encounter, he has given us warnings—watch out for this, beware of that. If we heed the warnings—keep his commandments—he will guide us safely home to him. If we insist on being disobedient—which our agency permits us to do—then we must suffer the consequences.

If you have parents who have taught you the commandments and who are encouraging you to be obedient, you are very fortunate. You're lucky if you have the "meanest mom and dad on the block," who insist you wait until you are sixteen years old to date or who always want to know where you are going, who you are with, and what time you will be home. You may be envious of friends who have been granted absolute freedom to do whatever they please. Nonetheless, such individuals are not only in great peril of losing their way but are justified in feeling abandoned and vulnerable.

So, what if? What if, after all the counsel, all the help from parents and leaders, you have still succumbed to Satan's siren call? I was recently invited to speak about fornication at a stake youth conference. While I was walking toward the stand to take my seat, someone thrust an envelope into my hand. There was a message scribbled on the back of it. It read, "Sister Marshall, please bring out the process of repentance strongly in your talk this evening. We have two young women in our stake who are pregnant out of wedlock, and each has tried to take her own life."

That is always painful to contemplate—that young people in trouble would feel so little hope as to try to destroy themselves. That kind of hopelessness suggests the depressed person does not understand the Atonement.

When Jesus submitted himself to the agony he experienced in Gethsemane, he was providing a way for each of us, personally, to be forgiven of our sins. If we don't take advantage of what he has done, then, in effect, we negate what he did for us and set his suffering aside.

The Savior extends his love to each of us, invites us to

repent of our wrongdoing, and promises us he will lift the burden of sin from our shoulders. He has explained, "For behold, I, God, have suffered these things for all, that they might not suffer if they would repent" (D&C 19:16). This promise applies even to those who have committed fornication.

Your bishop is the best friend you can have in such a situation. He is the one ordained of God to set you back on the right path. He can teach you how to repent and guide you through what may look dark and hopeless. If you are in this kind of circumstance, please have the courage to knock on his door and ask him for help. Repentance may seem scary, but it is the only way to get relief, dissolve the guilt, and begin the healing process.

When we read Alma 38:12, we need to consider the *whole* meaning of the verse: "And also see that ye bridle all your passions, *that ye may be filled with love*" (emphasis added). The Lord doesn't want to stifle our happiness. So, when he commands us to control our passions, he is not trying to deprive us of joy. Instead, he is trying to ensure that we will obtain the greatest joy possible — in this case, the joy that is available through sexual union. By waiting until marriage you will intensify the experience and spare yourself the pain associated with the sin of fornication.

The scriptures hint at what our reward will be if we truly love the Lord and demonstrate that love by keeping his commandments: "But as it is written, Eye hath not seen, nor ear heard, neither have entered into the heart of man, the things which God hath prepared for them that love him" (1 Corinthians 2:9).

Think about what you have read here; think about it really hard. Your whole "eternity" may hang in the balance. Start a revolution in your high school, your college apartment, your ward, your stake, and in your heart. Say no, and mean it. Make morality the "in" thing again.

CHAPTER 7

CONQUERING
AN UNWORTHY HABIT

BRAD WILCOX

"Dear Brother Wilcox," the letter began. "I appreciate the time you took to talk to me at youth conference, but I have to apologize. You complimented me on living the standards of the Church and called me an example, but I'm really not." The young man hadn't sent a picture with his letter, but I didn't need one to remember him. He was tall and handsome with a strong, athletic frame and a natural tan that made me envious. He was a student officer in his school and was active in seminary. From the outside, this guy looked pretty perfect to me. But, inside, things were different.

The letter continued: "For years I have struggled with something that I'm not proud of at all. It's a private, personal problem that I've tried so many times to overcome. I just get to where I've gone a long time without doing it and I'm feeling great, and then I blow it again. Is this cycle ever going to end? I'm so frustrated—I feel like pulling my hair out. I've been trying so long to be worthy—really worthy. You said I was strong, yet all I feel is weak and stupid. What should I do? Everything else in my life and at church is great. It's just this one thing. Please help me."

Masturbation—something that everyone seems to know about, many like to joke about, few will talk seriously about, and something that fewer still will address openly. Working with young people across the Church, I have come to realize that it is an all too common problem. I responded to my young friend's plea for help by making some suggestions. Perhaps some of the things I wrote to him may assist you if you are faced with the same struggle:

YOU ARE LOVED

Because of your inability to control this habit, you may have imagined that Heavenly Father is disgusted with you. On this subject, Elder Boyd K. Packer has stated, "I want you to know this, if you are struggling with this temptation and perhaps you have not quite been able to resist, the Lord still loves you" (*To Young Men Only* [Salt Lake City: The Church of Jesus Christ of Latter-day Saints, 1976], p. 4).

TURN TO GOD

Turn to heaven for help. Sometimes willpower alone is insufficient to make desired changes. Even sincere commitments can falter under pressure. Your understanding and strength alone may not be enough. You will need divine assistance.

One young person told me, "But I'm not worthy to pray anymore." Elder Richard G. Scott addressed those striving to overcome debilitating habits and said, "If your life is in disarray and you feel uncomfortable and unworthy to pray because you are not clean, don't worry. [Heavenly Father] already knows about all of that. He is waiting for you to kneel in humility and take the first few steps" ("True Friends that Lift," *Ensign,* Nov. 1988, p. 77).

In the scriptures we read, "I can do all things through Christ which strengtheneth me" (Philippians 4:13). That is a wonderful principle. Truly, the Savior will lend his strength to you. His enabling power begins where your willpower ends. After you try your hardest and do your best, Christ will make up the difference (see 2 Corinthians 12:9).

GO TO THE BISHOP

"But that's scary," young people tell me again and again when I encourage them to talk to their bishop. It can be frightening when we finally face our most personal weaknesses. Even the noble Adam and Eve were afraid after their transgression. They "went to hide themselves from the presence of the Lord God amongst the trees of the garden" (Moses 4:14). But could the trees hide them? No more effectively than silence, avoidance, and procrastination can conceal your deeds and thoughts from Heavenly Father.

Your bishop is the one who has been authorized to receive your confession and who can help you in your struggle. He can offer more than just friendly advice. He can provide true help, counsel, and guidance, and assist you to develop a positive plan of action to break bad habits, grow spiritually, and leave the past behind. He can become your ally in the effort you are making, and by some private signal between the two of you, strengthen and encourage you. You won't be in battle alone.

Some young people are concerned because the bishop also happens to be their dad or their uncle, a cousin, or a grandpa, or maybe even a close family friend. Having a relative for a bishop can sometimes make things a little awkward. But in most cases that won't be a problem for you or your bishop, no matter how closely you are related to him. But if

you simply can't go to your bishop, then go to your stake
president. He also can help you.

LEARN THE FACTS

The First Presidency has stated, "The Lord specifically
forbids certain behaviors, including . . . masturbation" (*For
the Strength of Youth* [Salt Lake City: The Church of Jesus
Christ of Latter-day Saints, 1990], p. 15). Elder Vaughn J.
Featherstone has written, "There is another sexual-related
personal problem which besets many young men and some
young women. . . . A few of our bishops feel that this personal
problem is not too serious because 'everyone does it.' This
is not true" (*A Generation of Excellence* [Salt Lake City: Bookcraft, 1975], p. 164). President Spencer W. Kimball declared:
"Masturbation, a rather common indiscretion, is not approved of the Lord nor of his church, regardless of what may
be said by others whose 'norms' are lower. Latter-day Saints
are urged to avoid this practice. Anyone fettered by this weakness should abandon the habit" (*President Kimball Speaks Out*
[Salt Lake City: Deseret Book, 1981], p. 10).

The world views the practice of masturbation as a harmless, natural sexual outlet that is a normal part of growing
up. The truth is that, for young men, nocturnal emissions and
the dreams that sometimes occur at the same time provide
a natural release for the body. When the body requires such
a release, it happens naturally, without stimulation. And
while there is no evidence that masturbation causes impo-
tence, pimples, or mental illness or that it interferes with
physical growth or normal development, there is evidence
that the practice carries with it some serious emotional and
spiritual consequences:

1. *Loss of the Spirit.* One teenager wrote: "The first time

I slipped back into my problem I actually felt the Spirit leave the room." The immediate consequence of *any* transgression is withdrawal of the Spirit. Instantly, we feel alone and miss the peace, comfort, safety, perspective, strength, and joy we usually feel.

2. *Selfishness.* President Spencer W. Kimball affirmed that "the Lord implanted the physical magnetism between the sexes for two reasons: for the propagation of the human race, and for the expression of that kind of love between man and wife that makes for true oneness" ("Guidelines to Carry Forth the Work of God in Cleanliness," *Ensign,* May 1974, p. 7). Masturbation fills neither purpose. It does not allow for procreation, and the only love involved is strictly a love of self.

3. *Subjection to a strong habit.* The difference between being in control of yourself and being controlled by a hated habit is the difference between freedom and slavery. Elder Boyd K. Packer warned: "A young man . . . might fondle himself and open that release valve. This you should not do, for if you do. . . . You will then be tempted again and again to release it. You can quickly be subjected to a habit, one that is not worthy" (*To Young Men Only,* p. 4).

4. *More serious problems.* Sexual self-indulgence and the fantasies that are often associated with it can lead to other sins. President Spencer W. Kimball specifically warned against such things as exhibitionism, petting, fornication, and homosexual practices (see *President Kimball Speaks Out,* p. 10). Aside from sexual problems, the secret practice of masturbation opens the door to rationalization, justification, and outright dishonesty. Because of embarrassment or fear, some lie during interviews, indicating that things are all right when they are not, or insist that the problem occurs less frequently

than it really does. Masturbation can create a reluctance to pray, participate with the family, or to be fully involved in the Church.

5. *Feelings of despair and guilt.* The world would have us believe that such feelings are of our own making or are imposed on us by an unreasonable Church standard. We know, however, that "despair cometh because of iniquity" (Moroni 10:22). Guilt is a spiritual signal. Todd Parker writes: "Guilt is to the spirit what pain is to the body. If you are playing basketball and twist an ankle, the physical pain gives you the signal, 'Stop! Don't do any more or you'll damage yourself further!' If you . . . feel guilty, the message is 'Stop! If you continue, you'll harm yourself spiritually' " (*High Fives and High Hopes: Favorite Talks Especially for Youth* [Salt Lake City: Deseret Book, 1990], p. 98).

6. *A compulsive cycle.* Those who behave in this way are often depressed by their lack of personal control. In an attempt to deal with the depression, they seek momentary relief and escape by repeating the very behavior that caused the depression in the first place. Feelings of depression then become worse and the desire for escape more intense. All too quickly, the participant finds himself caught in a downward cycle of compulsive behavior that is difficult to overcome.

7. *Lowered self-esteem.* LDS counselor A. Lynn Scoresby writes, "Self-abuse through masturbation will result in loss of self-esteem and feelings of self-doubt" (*In the Heart of a Child* [Salt Lake City: Bookcraft, 1987], p. 116). Most young people know that without having to be told. One boy wrote, "I made my goal last week. Let me tell you, I felt so good about myself. However, this week I messed up. My esteem went down like a bullet."

It is not likely you can overcome this habit without making a plan. Here are some suggestions:

1. *Be determined.* After learning the facts, make up your mind to do something about the problem. A seventeenth-century French general named Vicomte de Turenne was known for marching bravely into battle at the head of his troops. When asked if he was ever afraid, he admitted that sometimes he was but, he said, "I don't give in to the fear, but say to my body, 'Tremble, old carcass, but walk!' And my body walks" (*Reader's Digest,* Feb. 1992, p. 62). As you face your foe, you must show the same personal courage and determination.

Like stopping on a bicycle when you are approaching a red light at a dangerous intersection, you cannot hope to avoid problems by peddling and braking simultaneously. You must decide to stop, discontinue peddling, and finally, apply the brake. It's up to you. No one can do it for you. A young friend wrote: "This time, I am committed. Before, it's been like I wanted to change but somehow not really. I didn't want to give it up badly enough, but now I'm burning my bridges. There is no going back."

2. *Remove stumbling blocks.* We're all familiar with the advice given in Matthew 5:30 — "If thy right hand offend thee, cut it off" — yet too many are unclear what that statement really means. Todd Parker teaches: "A better definition of the word *offend* from the original Greek is 'cause to stumble.' In other words, if your eye is viewing something or your hand is tempted to touch something that would cause you to stumble spiritually, the Savior's advice is to get rid of the temptation. You should get away from it or not get near whatever it is that tempts you. He is suggesting that not only do we *not* do the sin, but also that we not even get near the

temptation, let alone the sin" (*High Fives and High Hopes*, p. 96).

Working on Sunday, listening to inappropriate music, swearing, looking at pornography, seeing R-rated movies — any R-rated movies — hanging around with friends who exert a bad influence, dating before sixteen or, having reached sixteen, pairing up and dating steadily, being idle, lying in bed when you are awake rather than getting up, taking extra long showers — these are all activities that can feed inappropriate thoughts and actions. Let's do as we are counseled by the Savior and cut out of our lives any activities that are causing us to stumble.

3. *Take charge of decisions.* Realistically, as hard as we try, we cannot eliminate every person, place, or thing associated with temptations. Sooner or later something we see or hear combines with certain feelings (depression, boredom, frustration) or thoughts ("I deserve to feel good," "Just this once won't hurt," "No one will know"), and resisting seems impossible.

But we are not puppets. We are free agents. Stop and think. Ask yourself, "Do I really need this? How will I feel afterwards? Is it worth it in the long run?" Avoid trading the lasting joy of what you want most for the momentary pleasure of what you want now.

4. *Set small goals.* A tangled heap of yarn is unraveled one knot at a time. A series of small, specific goals is often better than one big nebulous one. By accumulating a series of triumphs to build on, you will gain confidence to move forward.

Elder Boyd K. Packer writes, "You must leave [your body] alone long enough for it to slow down. Resisting is not easy. It will take weeks, even months" (*To Young Men Only,* p. 5).

Set small goals of abstinence. Start with a day, and then a week, then two. Perhaps you can mark goals and progress on a personal calendar. President Spencer W. Kimball wrote, "Certainly self-mastery is a continuous program—a journey, not a single start" (*The Miracle of Forgiveness* [Salt Lake City: Bookcraft, 1969], p. 210). It takes time to get our lives tangled up. They won't be straightened out in a single day.

5. *Distract yourself.* People often mistakenly believe that urges to give in to a bad habit just build and build until they accumulate devastating force and must be gratified. That's not true. Even the most intense urges fade if you simply distract yourself for a few minutes.

You have probably heard that singing a hymn is a good idea when you are tempted. You might also try reciting the Articles of Faith, reading good books, listening to uplifting music, or planning the details of a project you look forward to. It doesn't really matter what you choose to do; the idea is simply to keep temptation from taking center stage by focusing your mental spotlight elsewhere.

6. *Find a substitute.* We most easily break a destructive habit by replacing it with a good one. As with digging a hole in the backyard, if I don't want the dirt just to get pushed back in by the next rainstorm, I had better put something else—like cement—in place of the dirt.

After repenting and being forgiven of his sins, the brother of Jared was counseled by the Lord, "Go to work and build" (see Ether 2:15–16). That is wonderful instruction for us too. Work on building a worthy habit, and you'll feel as though you're adding something valuable to your life instead of just depriving yourself of a long-established indulgence.

7. *Stay busy and active.* One boy wrote: "When I messed up, it was the first time in weeks that I didn't have a full

schedule. I just had too much free time, and I was home by myself." Another wrote: "I was bored and lay down on my bed for just a moment. The temptation came because I was idle." These young men have learned that when dealing with an unworthy habit, the less time we give Satan, the less trouble he will be able to give us. Vigorous physical activity helps many resist temptation.

8. *Focus on doing positive things.* Participation in service projects, meetings, activities, sports, work, family home evening, and seminary will put your energies to good use and help you block out negative thoughts. One recently baptized young man was asked whether joining the Church had solved all his problems. He smiled, and said, "No, but it has left me with a lot less time to worry about them."

9. *Fast and read the scriptures.* Such practices as fasting and studying the scriptures temper desire and require us to develop self-mastery — mind over natural inclination. Beyond this, the scriptures are a source of great spiritual strength. President Ezra Taft Benson has promised that as we study the Book of Mormon, we will have greater power to resist temptations (see *A Witness and a Warning* [Salt Lake City: Deseret Book, 1988], pp. 21, 27, 36).

10. *Be with others.* Stay with groups. Be with good friends and with your family. Many young people tell me that when they are at a youth conference or attending Especially For Youth, they never have problems with an unworthy habit. Why? Not only do such events take place in an uplifting spiritual environment but the people who are involved are all of a like mind. A mind that is focused on others has a hard time focusing on selfish desires. Activities also keep you involved and reduce the amount of time you are able to spend alone.

Obviously, there are times when you will be alone. You can't bring everyone in your Sunday School class over to watch you go to sleep every night or to help you get ready every morning. If those are the times when you typically struggle, leave your bedroom door ajar or the bathroom door unlocked. That small gesture signals your intention and also provides a measure of caution. Knowing that you could instantly be entertaining a little brother or sister might be just enough incentive to keep you from entertaining tempting thoughts.

11. *Request a special blessing.* One letter I received said, "It's been three weeks now, and I have been doing great. It hasn't even been that much of a temptation because I got a blessing. It was so great — I'll never forget it." Just as Christ blessed eyes to see and ears to hear, I believe that we can be blessed with the strength to break unworthy habits.

"Oh sure," some might say. "I'm going to just run up to my dad or the bishop and ask him to bless me to stop doing this." Dads and priesthood leaders understand much more than you might think. If, however, you feel uncomfortable, you do not need to tell anyone the specific reason you are requesting a blessing. A sensitive priesthood holder will simply serve as a mouthpiece. You will receive your special blessing and counsel from an all-knowing and all-understanding Heavenly Father.

12. *Remember the Savior.* Members of the Church make covenants to remember Christ always (see D&C 20:77, 79). What better time to remember him than when we are struggling with an unworthy habit? Truman G. Madsen suggests: "Picture Christ and remember how you are bound to him. In the crisis, for example, when your temples thunder, imagine what you are tempted to do as if it were a large sledge hammer. See! See if you can stand at the cross and

by this act or indulgence swing that hammer on the nail. That will break your compulsive pattern and restore enough to your consciousness to enable you to cry out and mean, 'No!' " (*Christ and the Inner Life* [Salt Lake City: Bookcraft, 1978], p. 37).

13. *Celebrate private victories.* When you mow the lawn or do homework, people say, "Wonderful!" If you lose twenty pounds, people say, "Outstanding!" When you get your Duty to God or Young Women recognition award, everyone says, "Excellent!"

But what happens when you resist a personal temptation? Usually no one knows except God and you. So it's up to you to throw the party! Celebrate private victories as if your school had just taken state. Praise yourself. Reward yourself. Feel the Spirit that Heavenly Father sends. That peace and joy can reinforce and encourage you to make the same positive choice again in the future.

14. *Learn from past mistakes.* Although we don't seek, plan, or condone mistakes, they are a part of life and a part of any effort toward self-betterment. Perhaps that is why God has commanded that we partake of the sacrament so often — because he knows that we need plenty of chances to start over. No one learns to walk without falling down. Growth comes as we reflect on our choices, figure out what caused us to backslide, and then redouble our efforts. A lapse does not have to become a relapse.

Satan would have you dwell on your mistakes and wallow around in discouragement. Learn to examine your failures and try to determine what led up to the mistake, then set it aside, and move on. We must make the important distinction between our problems and ourselves. Failure is not a person, it is an incident, and it is always temporary in the context of the restored gospel of Jesus Christ.

Sometimes, especially as one gets older, this unworthy habit can be an indicator of a deeper problem such as low self-esteem, an inability to deal with pressure and stress, ineffective communication skills, or a lack of sufficient spirituality and testimony. If you are able to identify and take care of these kinds of problems, then changes in your behavior can become permanent.

15. *Keep perspective.* You will one day be able to legitimately express the feelings and impulses you are now struggling with. That will happen when you are married. Remember, your passions are not meant to be eliminated, expelled, or cut out of your life forever. They are, however, to be bridled and controlled (see Alma 38:12). Chastity is more than mere abstinence. It is getting to a happy and peaceful state of mind where you are not only able but also content to control your passions in preparation for the time of your marriage.

16. *You can make it.* Some of you may be thinking, "But I've done all that stuff before, and nothing ever changes." Don't be discouraged. Keep trying. You really can make it. One young man wrote: "I went and talked to my bishop. My life has taken a 180-degree turn for the good. I feel 100 percent better about myself. I can control my life." Another wrote: "I'm a few days short of three months free and clear. I saw my bishop, and I'm watching my weakness become a strength, just like it says in Ether 12:27."

This is a fight you can win for sure. You will feel more joy and satisfaction than you ever dreamed possible. You can shed the past and conquer this unworthy habit for good. Then, you'll feel like another young man who wrote: "I'm doing terrific. No problem at all any more. I was just called to be first assistant in the priest quorum and to be a youth missionary in our stake. I've finished reading Alma and am on Helaman 5 right now. I'm so happy I could burst. I never thought I could do it. I tried so many times before, but this time I finally did it. I found out that with God, nothing is impossible."

CHAPTER 8

WITHSTANDING
SEXUAL PRESSURE

JACK R. CHRISTIANSON

Withstanding the sexual pressures of our day is an incredible challenge. It is not just a challenge for the young and inexperienced. It is a pressure most people face, regardless of age. It is a challenge that can be overcome and must be met with strength and courage. For it seems that Satan has unleashed every vile practice in order to destroy and blind the sons and daughters of God. Surely, "the mists of darkness" spoken of by Father Lehi and in which Satan performs his labors, have descended over the earth as a thick blanket of confusion. Elder Boyd K. Packer of the Quorum of the Twelve Apostles described modern sexual pressures this way:

"The rapid, sweeping deterioration of values is characterized by a preoccupation—even an obsession—with the procreative act. Abstinence before marriage and fidelity within it are openly scoffed at—marriage and parenthood ridiculed as burdensome, unnecessary. Modesty, a virtue of a refined individual or society, is all but gone.

"The adversary is jealous toward all who have the power to beget life. He cannot beget life; he is impotent. He and those who followed him were cast out and forfeited the right to a mortal body. His angels even begged to inhabit the bodies of swine. (see Matt. 8:31) And the revelations tell us that 'he seeketh that all men might be miserable like unto himself' " (2 Ne 2:27). ("Our Moral Environment," *Ensign,* May 1992, p. 66).

Isn't that last line perceptive? The purpose of sexual pressure and other temptations is to make us miserable! Satan desires us to be sickeningly unhappy!

Elder Packer continues: "With ever fewer exceptions, what we see and read and hear have the mating act as a central theme. Censorship is forced offstage as a violation of individual freedom.

"That which should be absolutely private is disrobed and acted out center stage. In the shadows backstage are addiction, pornography, perversion, infidelity, abortion, and — the saddest of them all — incest and molestation. In company with them now is a plague of biblical proportion. And all of them are on the increase" ("Our Moral Environment," p. 66).

With so many voices in the world screaming at you to abandon your standards of morality and come and join in the party, how do you stand? Are you committed, determined, and straight? The purpose of this chapter is to share the principles that will help you to resist the temptations that come from every direction.

Many years ago I read an article by Elder Vaughn J. Featherstone that has had a great influence on me. I have used it often in sermons and speeches because its message is the key to withstanding the sexual pressures all around us. The story is about the son of King Louis XVI of France.

"King Louis had been taken from his throne and imprisoned. His young son, the prince, was taken by those who dethroned the king. They thought that inasmuch as the king's son was heir to the throne, if they could destroy him morally, he would never realize the great and grand destiny that life had bestowed upon him. [Sounds exactly like Satan's plan for us today! Destroy our morals and we never do realize who we are or why we're here.]

"They took him to a community far away, and there they exposed the lad to every filthy and vile thing that life could offer. They exposed him to foods the richness of which would quickly make him a slave to appetite. They used vile language around him constantly. They exposed him to lewd and lusting women. They exposed him to dishonor and distrust. He was surrounded 24 hours a day by everything that could drag the soul of a man as low as one could slip. For over six months he had this treatment—but not once did the young lad buckle under pressure. Finally, after intensive temptation, they questioned him. Why had he not submitted himself to these things—why had he not partaken? These things would provide pleasure, satisfy his lusts, and were desirable; they were all his. The boy said, 'I cannot do what you ask for I was born to be a king' " ("The King's Son," *New Era,* Nov. 1975, p. 35).

What a heroic response! The prince would not give in to all the pressures because he knew he had been born to be a king! You and I are also born to be kings and queens, priests and priestesses. Our Father is a King. He is the King of kings—the King of all things. He is God.

All our children are daughters, and we desire to remind them of who they are and for what purpose they were born, so, hanging on the wall beside our front door is a framed plaque that reads: "I was born to be a queen." Some may scoff and say that this approach to withstanding sexual pressure is too idealistic or too simple. But, as far as I'm concerned, it is the "very key" to withstanding the pressures exerted by the outside world.

Elder Boyd K. Packer has also stated: "You are a child of God. He is the father of your spirit. Spiritually you are of noble birth, the offspring of the King of Heaven. Fix that truth in your mind and hold to it. However many generations in your mortal ancestry, no matter what race or people you represent, the pedigree of your spirit can be written on a single line. You are a child of God! . . .

"Within your body is the power to beget life, to share in creation. The only legitimate expression of the power is within the covenant of marriage. The worthy use of it is the very key to your happiness. Do not use the power prematurely, not with anyone. The misuse of it cannot be made right by making it popular.

"Your spirit operates through your mind, but cultivating your intellect is not enough. Reason alone will neither protect nor redeem you. Reason nourished by faith can do both" ("To Young Men and Women," *Ensign,* May 1989, p. 54).

There has never been an idea more destructive to happiness or one that has produced more sorrow and pain and destroyed more families than the idea that we are not the children of God but are instead only advanced animals following and giving in to every urge and desire.

With the knowledge that you are a son or daughter of the heavenly King rooted firmly within you, it is possible to understand the whys of complete chastity. Then you will be fortified with the courage and strength that will enable you to withstand the "mists of darkness" that shroud the world.

The First Presidency has declared: "A correct understanding of the divinely appointed roles of men and women will fortify all against sinful practices. Our only real safety, physically and spiritually, lies in keeping the Lord's commandments" (14 Nov. 1991).

This correct understanding can help each person comprehend why sexual intimacy is so sacred and why the Lord requires self-control and purity before marriage and full fidelity after marriage. We begin to understand why the physical relationship between a husband and a wife can be beautiful and sacred. This relationship is ordained of God for two purposes: the procreation of children and the expression of love within a marriage (see *For the Strength of Youth* [Salt Lake City: The Church of Jesus Christ of Latter-day Saints, 1990], pp. 14–15).

I have often heard young people ask: "Why does a little piece of paper make such a difference? Why in one minute are sexual relations not okay and the next minute, after a brief ceremony, they are okay?"

Many seem to feel that as long as they are "safe" and a pregnancy does not occur or a disease is not contracted, then everything is okay. You need to understand that having sexual relations outside of marriage is not wrong simply because a pregnancy may occur or because a deadly disease, like AIDS, may be contracted. Those are definitely two of the reasons you need to be morally clean, but they are not the major reasons. The most important reasons run far deeper, and if you understand them, that understanding will help you withstand sexual pressures.

1. One reason God is God is that he possesses the power to create and to give life. He possesses a "continuation of the seeds forever and ever." He has placed within his children the same power—a power we possess in a limited form here on earth and which he has promised he will bestow in eternity on those who keep his commandments. Obviously, there are

many people who, because of physical limitations, cannot create life. But most human beings can participate in the act of creation. To act as a creator simply requires permission from the giver of the law. The Lord has explained:

"And again, verily I say unto you, if a man marry a wife by my word, which is my law, and by the new and everlasting covenant, and it is sealed unto them by the Holy Spirit of promise, by him who is anointed, unto whom I have appointed this power and the keys of this priesthood; and it shall be said unto them — Ye shall come forth in the first resurrection; and if it be after the first resurrection, in the next resurrection; and shall inherit thrones, kingdoms, principalities, and powers, dominions, all heights and depths — then shall it be written in the Lamb's Book of Life, that he shall commit no murder whereby to shed innocent blood, and if ye abide in my covenant, and commit no murder whereby to shed innocent blood, it shall be done unto them in all things whatsoever my servant hath put upon them, in time, and through all eternity; and shall be of full force when they are out of the world; and they shall pass by the angels, and the gods, which are set there, to their exaltation and glory in all things, as hath been sealed upon their heads, which glory shall be a fulness and a continuation of the seeds forever and ever. . . .

"Verily, verily, I say unto you, except ye abide my law ye cannot attain to this glory" (D&C 132:19, 21).

2. While describing the condition of his people to his son Moroni, the prophet Mormon painted a picture of the depths of depravity to which the Nephites and Lamanites had sunk. It sickens us to read how little they valued human life and how cruel they had become. Yet in this depiction, a wonderful lesson on the value of chastity and virtue is taught:

"And the husbands and fathers of those women and children they have slain; and they feed the women upon the flesh of their husbands, and the children upon the flesh of their fathers; and no water, save a little, do they give unto them.

"And notwithstanding this great abomination of the Lamanites, it doth not exceed that of our people in Moriantum. For behold, many of the daughters of the Lamanites have they taken prisoners; and after depriving them of that which was most dear and precious above all things, which is chastity and virtue —

"And after they had done this thing, they did murder them in a most cruel manner, torturing their bodies even unto death; and after they have done this, they devour their flesh like unto wild beasts, because of the hardness of their hearts; and they do it for a token of bravery" (Moroni 9:8–10).

Why are chastity and virtue more "dear and precious" than "all things"? Why are they of more value than life itself? Because they are the very source of life! Thinking, breathing, feeling human beings are brought into existence through the magnificent act of procreation. Nevertheless, as Elder Packer has said: "The source of life is now relegated to the level of unwed pleasure, bought and sold and even defiled in satanic rituals. Children of God can willfully surrender to their carnal nature and, without remorse, defy the laws of morality and degrade themselves even below the beasts. If we pollute our fountains of life, there will be penalties 'exquisite' and 'hard to bear' (see D&C 19:15), more than all of the physical pleasure ever could be worth" ("Our Moral Environment," pp. 67–68). Simply put, "Wickedness never was happiness" (Alma 41:10).

3. Alma told his son Corianton: "Know ye not, my son, that these things are an abomination in the sight of the Lord;

yea, most abominable above all sins save it be the shedding of innocent blood or denying the Holy Ghost?" (Alma 39:5).

Why would the misuse of these sexual powers be next to murder in seriousness? When an individual murders someone, the murderer forces the victim's spirit out of his or her body. That leaves the body and spirit separated until the resurrection. The murderer has presumed to interfere with another's agency and has forced the murdered person into the spirit world, thus depriving the murdered person of any further earthly experience and leaving a wake of sorrow and pain for those who remain in mortality.

When two people misuse their creative powers and a pregnancy occurs outside a regularly constituted family, a spirit is forced to leave the premortal existence and enter into the newly created body. In this way too an individual's agency is tampered with and God's plan is violated.

Because of eternal ramifications, the Lord has reserved to himself the prerogative to decide the proper time for his children to either enter or leave mortality. It is God who "hath made of one blood all nations of men for to dwell on all the face of the earth, and hath determined the times before appointed, and the bounds of their habitation" (Acts 17:26). The Lord simply has forbidden the taking of spirits out of bodies and the bringing of spirits into bodies without his permission, saying: "Thou shalt love thy neighbor as thyself. Thou shalt not steal; neither commit adultery, nor kill, nor do anything like unto it" (D&C 59:6). Furthermore, he has reserved his most severe punishments for those who presume to trifle with the sanctity of life.

A marriage certificate is a permission slip, so to speak, from the Lord, that allows us to participate with him in his plan to "multiply, and replenish the earth" (Moses 2:28) —

to provide bodies for his spirit children. And it is only in marriage that men and women are authorized so to act and to express their love in the most intimate ways.

4. We participate in the gospel of Jesus Christ by making covenants. The covenants are entered into by participating in ordinances and thereby making promises, which we are asked to renew frequently in various ways. For example, by being baptized we "witness before him [Christ] that [we] have entered into a covenant with him" (Mosiah 18:10) to take upon us his name, to always remember him, and to keep his commandments. Then, weekly, we renew that covenant by partaking of the sacrament (see D&C 20:77, 79).

The order, then, is to make a covenant, participate in an ordinance, and then renew the covenant. Should marriage, "the new and everlasting covenant" (D&C 132:19), be any different? We make a sacred covenant with our spouse to give ourselves completely to each other. We are sealed or married by proper authority (the ordinance). Then, we renew the covenant we have made to give all that we have and to be "one flesh." How do we renew the covenant? One of the ways is to express our love by giving ourselves completely to our spouse in a sexual relationship. As Elder Jeffrey R. Holland has said, the sexual union between a husband and a wife is in a sense a "sacrament," or renewal of the marriage covenant ("Of Souls, Symbols, and Sacraments," *Brigham Young University 1987–88 Devotional and Fireside Speeches* [Provo: Brigham Young University Press, 12 Jan. 1988], pp. 74–85).

The violation of the law of chastity, then, is a violation of one of the most sacred covenants or sacraments that men and women ever enter into while in mortality.

Those are some of the reasons why the Lord has condemned any sexual relationship outside the bonds of marriage. Happiness can never come from such relationships or acts because participants in immorality "are without God in the world, and they have gone contrary to the nature of God; therefore, they are in a state contrary to the nature of happiness" (Alma 41:11).

Now that we have a better understanding of "why" morality is so important, we are prepared for a few suggestions on "how" to withstand sexual pressures.

As you read these few suggestions, I hope you will not dismiss them because they are so simple. I understand most of you will have heard these things all your life. That's the point! We must now learn "not only to *say,* but to *do* according to that which I [the Lord] have written" (D&C 84:57; emphasis added).

OUR DIVINE HERITAGE

The first defense against sexual pressure is to truly believe that we are the sons and daughters of God. We must then try to understand the whys of chastity—that chastity is more than merely avoiding pregnancy or disease but is a matter instead of "souls" (life), "symbols" (commitment to intimate relationships), and "sacraments" (commitments to the making and keeping of sacred covenants) ("Of Souls, Symbols, and Sacraments," pp. 74–85).

PRAYER

Then we must involve ourselves in the most basic of religious practices. We must learn to pray. Not just learn to say prayers but truly to pray. "Verily, verily, I say unto you, ye must watch and pray always, lest ye be tempted by the devil, and ye be led away captive by him. . . . Behold, verily, verily, I say unto you, ye must watch and pray always lest ye enter into temptation; for Satan desireth to have you, that he may sift you as wheat" (3 Nephi 18:15, 18).

Imagine the effect it would have if, while preparing to go out on a date, every young man and young woman would pray for the strength to withstand temptation.

CHARITY

What should we pray for? May I suggest that we learn to pray with all our energy of heart for the gift of charity. I believe there is a direct relationship between charity and chastity. "Charity ... thinketh no evil, and rejoiceth not in iniquity but rejoiceth in the truth ... [and] endureth all things" (Moroni 7:45). Charity is the "pure love of Christ, and it endureth forever" (Moroni 7:47).

But charity is a gift and must be asked for—and not just asked for casually. "Wherefore, my beloved brethren, pray unto the Father with all the energy of heart, that ye may be filled with this love, which he hath bestowed upon all who are true followers of his Son, Jesus Christ; that ye may become the sons of God; that when he shall appear we shall be like him, for we shall see him as he is; that we may have this hope; that we may be purified even as he is pure" (Moroni 7:48). We must pray for purity with "all the energy of heart." That's one thing we must be praying for in every situation.

When we have prayed for and received this gift of charity (which must happen over and over in our lives), and when we are letting "virtue garnish our thoughts unceasingly," something wonderful happens to us. "Let thy bowels also be full of charity towards all men, and to the household of faith, and let virtue garnish thy thoughts unceasingly; then shall thy confidence wax strong in the presence of God; and the doctrine of the priesthood shall distil upon thy soul as the dews from heaven.

"The Holy Ghost shall be thy constant companion, and
thy scepter an unchanging scepter of righteousness and truth;
and thy dominion shall be an everlasting dominion and without compulsory means it shall flow unto thee forever and
ever" (D&C 121:45–46).

If we are virtuous, our confidence will be strong, we will
have the Holy Ghost, and thus we will see clearly. And then
we can resist evil.

CONTROLLING OUR THOUGHTS

When we do not have charity and thus lose control of
our thoughts, we put ourselves in danger of transgression:
"And he that looketh upon a woman to lust after her shall
deny the faith, and shall not have the Spirit; and if he repents
not he shall be cast out" (D&C 42:23). What this scripture
means is that lustful thoughts deprive us of the companionship of the Holy Ghost, and without that, our testimonies
falter. Then, unable to see things clearly (see Jacob 4:13) and
blinded by desire, we might surrender to our carnal desires
and transgress. If we don't repent, we will be cast out and,
as it says in Doctrine and Covenants 63:16, we "shall fear."
Rather than have confidence, we will fear! We must pray
specifically for charity. Elder Marvin J. Ashton has com-
mented: "Real charity is not something you give away; it is
something that you acquire and make a part of yourself. And
when the virtue of charity becomes implanted in your heart,
you are never the same again" ("The Tongue Can Be a Sharp
Sword," *Ensign*, May 1992, p. 19).

AVOID EVIL

Speaking of young Latter-day Saint men and women, President Spencer W. Kimball has said: "The devil knows how to destroy them. He knows, young men and women, that he cannot tempt you to commit adultery immediately, but he knows too that he can soften you up by lewd associations, vulgar talk, immodest dress, sexy movies, and so on. He knows too that if he can get them to drink or if he can get them into his 'necking and petting' program, the best boys and the best girls will finally succumb and will fall" (*The Miracle of Forgiveness* [Salt Lake City: Bookcraft, 1969], pp. 230–31). We must avoid situations in which either we have had trouble in the past or we know we could have trouble in the future. We must avoid the pitfalls!

President Kimball has also counseled that we avoid long, lusty, passionate kissing: "Kissing has been prostituted and has been degenerated to develop and express lust instead of affection, honor, and admiration. To kiss in casual dating is asking for trouble. What do kisses mean when given out like pretzels or robbed of sacredness?" (Spencer W. Kimball, in Sydney Australia Area Conference Report, Feb. 29, 1976, p. 55).

The pamphlet *For the Strength of Youth* contains many practical suggestions on how to resist sexual pressures. In one place it deals with modesty in dress and appearance. "Servants of God have always counseled his children to dress modestly to show respect for him and for themselves. Because the way you dress sends messages about yourself to others and often influences the way you and others act, you should dress in such a way as to bring out the best in yourself and those around you. However, if you wear an immodest bathing suit because it's 'the style,' it sends a message that you are using your body to get attention and approval, and that modesty is not important" (p. 8).

The scriptures contain many examples of those who have succeeded in standing up to the pressures and who were conditioned to "shake at the appearance of sin" (Nephi 4:3). If we are to succeed, we need to run from evil and not be afraid of what others may think of us. I realize how difficult that is, but don't we run from things that would destroy us physically? Then why not run from evil—that which will destroy us spiritually?

SHUN PORNOGRAPHY

President Gordon B. Hinckley has given us some wonderful counsel on the subject of pornography. He said: "You cannot afford in any degree to become involved with pornography, whatever its form. You simply cannot afford to become involved in immoral practices—or to let down the bars of sexual restraint. The emotions that stir within you which make boys attractive to girls and girls attractive to boys are part of a divine plan, but they must be restrained, subdued, and kept under control, or they will destroy you and make you unworthy of many of the great blessings which the Lord has in store for you" ("A Chosen Generation," *Ensign,* May 1992, p. 71).

What greater example could be found of successfully withstanding sexual pressure than Joseph of Egypt? From the days of my youth, his story has inspired me. Joseph is one of my greatest heroes. He knew he was a son of our heavenly King. He avoided the "pitfalls," and when the time came to withstand the pressure, his only concern was not to "sin against God" (Genesis 39:9).

As you know, Joseph had been ripped away from his

beloved father Jacob and sold as a slave into Egypt by his jealous brothers. Even in slavery the Lord was with Joseph, and the young man prospered. With the continued blessing of the Lord, Joseph rose to a position of authority in the household of Potiphar, second only to Potiphar himself. As Joseph carried out his duties in his master's house, Potiphar's wife began to lust after this handsome, strong, young Israelite. "And it came to pass after these things, that his master's wife cast her eyes upon Joseph; and she said, Lie with me.

"But he refused, and said unto his master's wife, Behold, my master wotteth not what is with me in the house, and he hath committed all that he hath to my hand;

"There is none greater in this house than I; neither hath he kept back any thing from me but thee, because thou art his wife: how then can I do this great wickedness, and sin against God?

"And it came to pass, as she spake to Joseph day by day, that he hearkened not unto her, to lie by her, or to be with her.

"And it came to pass about this time, that Joseph went into the house to do his business; and there was none of the men of the house there within.

"And she caught him by his garment, saying, Lie with me: and he left his garment in her hand, and fled, and got him out" (Genesis 39:6–12).

Joseph ran!

Joseph remembered. He knew he was a son of God. He knew the whys of chastity. He knew why it was not just wrong but why it was "great wickedness" to express his sexuality outside of marriage. He did not want to disappoint his Father, his heavenly King.

Oh, that each of us might respond to the sexual pressures

in our lives as Joseph did! Then the "mists of darkness" would begin to fade and our lights would shine through the darkness of this sin-stained world to bless not only our own lives but the lives of many of our King's sons and daughters. We are all born to be kings and queens. We all need help to stay on the well-lighted path that leads to the "tree whose fruit was desirable to make one happy" (1 Nephi 8:10).

REPENTANCE

There is little doubt that some readers will have struggled and fallen at times or given in to the enormous weight of today's sexual pressures. Please, dear reader, believe that there is hope. You have not gone too far. You can return. Elder Boyd K. Packer has taught us that there is hope ("Our Moral Environment," p. 68):

"In the battle of life, the adversary takes enormous numbers of prisoners, and many who know of no way to escape and are pressed into his service. Every soul confined to a concentration camp of sin and guilt has a key to the gate. The adversary can not hold them if they know how to use it. The key is labeled *repentance*. The twin principles of repentance and forgiveness exceed in strength the awesome power of the adversary.

"I know of no sins connected with the moral standard for which we cannot be forgiven. I do not exempt abortion. The formula is stated in forty words: 'Behold, he who has repented of his sins, the same is forgiven, and I, the Lord, remember them no more.

" 'By this ye may know if a man repenteth of his sins— behold, he will confess them and forsake them' " (D&C 58:42–43).

However long and painful the process of repentance,

there is hope. There is hope through the atoning sacrifice of Jesus Christ. There is hope that through understanding the "whys" of chastity and putting into practice the "hows," we can withstand the sexual pressures of our modern world. There is hope because as children of our heavenly King, we were born to be kings and queens.

CHAPTER 9

WE BELIEVE IN BEING VIRTUOUS

ELAINE CANNON

We believe in being virtuous because virtue is what enables us, in this life, to enjoy the constant companionship of the Holy Ghost. It is his influence that insulates us against the evils of the world and that permits us to discern what is truth and what is a lie, to distinguish between friends and enemies, to understand what is right and what is wrong, to sense the presence of danger, and to feel the flood of sweeping assurance that Jesus is the Christ—that he is alive and that he is waiting to be gracious to us.

We believe in being virtuous because virtue is what will qualify us to enjoy the companionship of the Lord Jesus Christ and God our Heavenly Father in the life after this.

Virtue is purity, goodness, and moral rectitude. To be virtuous is to be innocent, clean, and chaste. One who is virtuous attempts to do what is right and endeavors to keep God's commandments.

To be virtuous is to resist temptations to do evil or behave in any way that would stifle your spiritual growth or that would harm your physical body, which is the temple that houses your eternal spirit.

Virtue is the quality that makes you want to live after the

114

manner of the Lord Jesus Christ—our leader, teacher, and example, our Savior and Redeemer. And virtue is one of the characteristics of goodness that will qualify you for eternal life.

You may feel as though you are going to live forever. That is one of the attributes of youth—a sense that death is a long way off, something to be considered at a much later date. But look around you. Young people are moving on through the veil of death all the time! Ready or not, you (any one of us) could be taken from this life in an instant. It would be well to ask yourself this question: "If I were taken now, how would the Lord evaluate my life and what would happen to me?"

To emphasize the importance of being virtuous, a dramatic presentation entitled "The Flight of Life" was made to the youth of one ward during a standards night program. The youth boarded an imaginary airplane for a festive flight to some unnamed destination and were asked to pretend they were the victims of a crash in which there were no survivors. The young men and young women proceeded into "Heaven's Waiting Room." There, a priesthood leader dressed in white clothing greeted them and extended a welcome as he explained the organization of God's heaven and described the kind of people who will ultimately enjoy dwelling there. He stated that only those who are pure and virtuous would be invited into the presence of the Father, citing the scripture "no unclean thing can dwell with God" (1 Nephi 10:21). Then he asked for a show of hands. "All of you who would like to go to the celestial kingdom, raise your hand."

Of course, all raised their hands except one twelve-year-old young woman seated on the front row.

"Mary Nell, don't you want to go to the celestial kingdom?"

"I can't," explained the girl sadly. "My mother told me to come straight home."

Don't you imagine that is the same instruction we were given by our heavenly parents as they sent us forth to enter mortality and experience life on planet Earth? "Come straight home, beloved spirit!"

But returning home just isn't going to be possible if you aren't virtuous. You have perhaps learned that oil and water don't mix. Similarly, the blessings of heaven cannot be obtained by those who are unclean—virtue and vice don't mix, either.

Preparing yourself to return home to Heavenly Father is something like working to pass your classes so you can move on to the next level in school. To get from one grade to another or from high school to college, you need to accumulate a certain number of credits. In the school of life you keep the commandments so that you can enjoy the continuing companionship and guidance of the Holy Ghost—so you can qualify for a mission and temple endowments and marriage, and eventually, so you can gain admission into the celestial kingdom.

It is not virtuous to shoplift, to lie, to cheat on tests or interviews, to pass damaging rumors about others, to be disrespectful of your parents, whom God has said you should honor. It is not virtuous to use profanity, pursue pornographic entertainment, or dress or behave immodestly. It is not virtuous to engage in sexual activity of any kind until after you are legally married. That is God's will, no matter how the world may view or promote premarital sex. The standard the

Lord has established is one of chastity and abstinence until the right time.

Richard was talking with his mother about how much he loved Sherry. The two young people were in the same seminary class and had many of the same interests. There was heavy chemistry at work in their relationship, too. Neither was prepared for the strong feelings they began to feel for each other or for the desire that had begun to tug at them to express their affection. They'd never felt like that before, and it was wonderful and a little scary all at the same time. They knew the rules, but they couldn't understand the rules when it *seemed so right, so natural,* for them to be as close as possible to each other.

"Son, waiting until after marriage to share your bodies and physical intimacies with each other is what God expects of you and Sherry. Regardless of what others may say or do, you must not surrender to your desires. Why? Because if you submit to sexual drives out of wedlock, you step onto Satan's turf. He *wants* you to fall. He wants to render you ineligible for a mission or for temple marriage. He wants you to be denied the spirit of the Holy Ghost and the precious gifts of that companionship. Self-control—spirit over body—is what you should think about. Reach for God's help to keep his plan, not Satan's."

Richard's mother wasn't just lecturing. She loved her son and was making an earnest effort to help him avoid a tragic disaster in his life. She praised his admirable qualities and reminded him of his potential. Together, they read his patriarchal blessing and noted the promises and cautions contained in it. She gave him good advice about building a friendship with Sherry—a friendship that would last all their lives, a friendship free from sin or guilt. She explained that sin isn't hurtful because it is forbidden but rather that sin is forbidden because it is hurtful!

Richard and Sherry kept their virtue, and though they remained friends, circumstances led them apart. Each eventually married someone else. Then one day, years later, Sherry sat across a desk from Richard. He was now her bishop, and she had been called to be the ward relief society president. They would be working closely with each other. Each was grateful to be able to do so with a clear conscience, without shame of any kind. They were qualified to serve the Lord and the people of their ward, and nothing in their former relationship lurked in their memories to hinder their effectiveness. They had been blessed by being virtuous.

Being virtuous also brings *immediate* rewards. Every time you succeed in keeping a commandment of God, you get a good feeling. Your determination to do right becomes stronger. You build moral fiber that will protect you against future temptations.

Think of Joseph who was sold as a slave to one of the most powerful leaders of Egypt. Potiphar found in Joseph a faithful servant and entrusted him with many responsibilities. Joseph was loyal to his master and performed his duties faithfully. But Potiphar's wife was a seductress who used all her feminine charms and enticements to get the handsome young Israelite to succumb to her sexual advances. He continually declined her invitations, saying, "How then can I do this great wickedness, and sin against God?" Then one day, as he was resisting yet another of her immoral invitations, she took hold of his garment. Determined to preserve his virtue, Joseph turned from her and "got him[self] out," fleeing both her clutches and the consequences of immorality (Genesis 39:1–13).

That is one of the great stories in the scriptures, and reading it many thousands of years after it occurred, we remember Joseph for his integrity. Confronted with such a test today, how would you respond? It is quite likely that unless you have made up your mind beforehand and have already decided what you would do in a similar situation, you will not have the determination to resist. If, however, you have previously declared your faith in God and made a decision to remain morally clean, and if you don't entertain fantasies or deliberately put yourself in the way of temptation, you too can resist evil.

Here are some famous last lines: "Whew! I made it! I am safely graduated, safely home from 'Prom Night,' safely ordained, safely through the bishop's interview, safely on a mission, safely married in the temple, safely finished with mortality, and safely encircled in the arms of Jesus!"

Famous (safe) last lines may be spoken after a lifetime of virtuous living. A virtuous life, well lived, will ensure happiness now and eternal life hereafter.

The age you are as you read this isn't as important as how *together* you are, how close to the Lord you are, and how guided by the Holy Ghost you are. You are a child of God. Therefore, you are "somebody." How intensely does God, your Heavenly Father, love you?

You are part of an exciting plan, a plan that stretches from premortal life through your turn on earth and into the reaches of all eternity.

You have a destiny—a glorious purpose for living.

You are boosted forward and supported along the way by your membership in the Lord's true church—The Church of Jesus Christ of Latter-day Saints.

You have been blessed with the gift of the Holy Ghost to guide you, warn you, and teach you.

You live during a time when there is a flood of knowledge, when you have a whole host of good options for how you will live your life.

You are supported by the leaders of the Church—both local and general.

You have full access to eternal principles in the holy scriptures.

As long as you keep your hand on the iron rod, your feet on the path of righteousness, and your heart close to God, Satan will have no power to inhibit your progress.

Satan is interested in destroying you because he is at war with the kingdom of God on earth. You are on God's team. You have a certain destiny to prepare yourself to spread the gospel. Being virtuous is keeping spiritually fit for the *great* battle.

You train for being virtuous. You train for it just as you would train to excel in any worthwhile endeavor by taking skiing, music, or sewing lessons or by working with weights to build your body.

What's so great about virtue? It is its own reward. Wholesomeness, purity, and goodness smooth out the path that leads to forever. If you live a virtuous life, there will be fewer disappointments, delays, and detours to negotiate on the road of life. That doesn't mean you will be spared all pain or temptation. It does mean that you will have the strength to overcome.

History and experience both confirm that neither individuals nor nations have any peace or experience much joy when virtue is lost. But what about you? Why virtue? What's in it for you?

Well, first of all, you need to be virtuous because God said so. Why do you suppose God said so? Because wickedness never was happiness and never will be (see Alma 41:10). You see, heaven and happiness just can't happen among sinners — among thieves and lecherous rogues, among abusers and power mongers, and among all the rest who cultivate anti-Christ qualities.

The pure joy of God's love is not to be found among lustful people who scoff at God's moral laws. Immoral persons choose to ignore the eternal ramifications of their behavior. They go along, participating in illicit sexual activities, making babies, falling into and out of intimate relationships, participating in deviant behavior of all kinds, contracting a variety of sexual diseases, and suffering the dissatisfaction and restlessness that are the products of their behavior. Though some people don't know any better, you do! Avoid such anguish no matter what!

To be virtuous is a wonderful condition for a young person to be in. When you have clean hands and a pure heart, when you are obedient to God's commandments, and when you are able to ignore the temptations of the world, you enjoy a wonderful sense of peace and well-being.

On the other hand, immorality destroys the mind, the heart, the body, and eventually the soul. Individuals who seek only to satisfy their immoral appetites are generally selfish, uncaring, and profoundly unhappy. There is a longing in them that can never be satisfied. They have separated themselves from the Spirit of the Lord and, unless they repent, they are in jeopardy of losing the eternal blessings reserved for the righteous.

How do you become virtuous? Virtue is not hereditary. Virtue is not a gene thing. It helps to be reared in a close, protected family circle where God's truths are taught and virtuous living is a constant goal. But even if you are in that kind of fortunate situation, you, yourself, will still have to choose to be virtuous. Like the process of finding a testimony of Jesus Christ, the pursuit of virtue is an individual thing. Moreover, you cannot put virtue on and take it off like a convenient cloak. You can't break the commandments in one way or another on Saturday night and then show up at the sacrament table on Sunday, presuming to participate in sacred priesthood ordinances. That isn't right! For one thing, such behavior is a violation of the trust the Lord has placed in you. If you have ever tried to live that kind of lie, you know how uncomfortable a guilty conscience can make you—the still small voice becomes a roar of condemnation. Only absolute humility and repentance will ease that kind of pain. If you think you can live both ways and program your conscience out, you are suffering from denial and will eventually find you can't continue to live like that forever.

Virtue is not contagious. It is earned. It helps to choose good friends who have similar ideals and goals. It is easier to do what is right when everyone else is.

Virtue is achieved daily (by seconds, minutes, hours) by adhering to the way of light and life according to the Creator's plan for us.

Young people often ask, "What does anything anybody had to say two thousand years ago have to do with me?" The answer is loud and clear. Everything! If you want to boggle your mind, consider what was said more than four thousand years ago to Adam and Eve! They were also given standards of behavior by God. Such standards are the rules of the game of life, tips from the owner's manual.

How do you remain virtuous?

Hang true. You know, like a carpenter's plumb line hangs true. You can't pull up carrots if you plant corn. You can't pretend to be something you are not. Remember, you have made promises to God—promises when you were baptized, when you have partaken of the sacrament, when you received the priesthood. Be true to your commitments, and the Lord will bless you.

Hang in there. Don't allow somebody else's lack of virtue or rebellion to ruin your life! Maybe they don't understand, but you do. So keep moving in the direction *you* are supposed to go, doing what *you* are supposed to do. Stay alert for the potholes along your particular highway of life.

Hang loose. Keep calm. Relax, but don't give in, give up, or create trouble for others. The Lord has promised that if we will let virtue garnish our thoughts unceasingly, our confidence will grow strong in his presence (see D&C 121:45). He will help you, so why be uptight and self-conscious? You have a personal witness that Jesus lives. It is his *mission* to help you! Remember, he said, "For behold, this is my work and my glory—to bring to pass the immortality and eternal life of man" (Moses 1:39).

Hold on. Hold on to dear life. Fasten your seat belt. Put on your life jacket, your helmet, your running shoes or cleats. And keep your hand in the Lord's, too. Life comes just once to a customer.

One day I answered a knock at our door and was surprised to see a friend of our family standing there. He was supposed to be in Europe on a mission. What was he doing home now? He lunged through the door and fell into my arms, sobbing. "Oh, why did I do it? Why did I do it?" he wailed. When he was finally able to talk, he told me that within thirty hours of his arrival in the mission field, he had committed a sexual sin with a young woman he met. He had confessed, been excommunicated, and sent home in dishonor. His parents were out of town when he arrived home, so he had come at once to our house. As we talked, he asked a significant question. "If I couldn't resist temptation when I had the Holy Ghost, how will I ever make things right now? How will I get through the rest of my life?"

You see, if you are excommunicated, the blessings of Church membership, including the gift of the Holy Ghost, are removed from your life. This young man had already begun to sense what that feels like. He was heartbroken, miserable, and desperate, and he looked forward with dread to all the things he would have to confront. He wondered if he would have the strength to repent and eventually recover his membership in the Church.

As I listened to his story and observed his sorrow, my heart went out to him. He was paying a heavy price for the fleeting moment of gratification he experienced when he surrendered his virtue.

The Lord has revealed this important principle to us: "There is a law, irrevocably decreed in heaven before the foundations of this world, upon which all blessings are predicated—and when we obtain any blessing from God, it is by obedience to that law upon which it is predicated" (D&C 130:20–21).

To understand how this principle works, think about the world we live in. For example, if you want to attend college, you must keep your grades up and graduate from high school. Obey the law—reap the benefit. Similarly, if you want the blessings of a temple marriage, you must live in such a way as to be able to pass the temple recommend interview. The blessings based on obedience to the law of chastity are particularly desirable and include freedom of conscience, freedom from sexually transmitted diseases, increased spirituality, the privilege of going to the temple or of going on a mission, and the joy of becoming a worthy parent.

To ensure the greatest amount of happiness in this life, you must learn to bridle all your passions and appetites. Bad habits enslave us and restrict our freedom. We must learn to control such things as sexual desires; a tendency to overeat; addictions to tobacco, alcohol, or drugs; the tendency to lie, cheat, or steal; the use of pornography; or even the practice of wasting time. By living in harmony with gospel principles you will be filled with the Holy Ghost and be further strengthened to resist temptation.

We believe in being virtuous because it is the best way to live—for now and forever!

CHAPTER 10

MODERN MEDIA AND MORALITY

RANDAL A. WRIGHT

When I was fourteen years old, the Church built a new chapel in the area of Texas where I was living. That was during the time when the members helped in the construction of buildings, so my friends and I loved to go down and watch. One of the last projects was to pour a cement base for the steeple. After the contractors left, one of my friends suggested that we write our names and the date in the wet cement. He reasoned that the steeple would cover the names but that in the future we could tell our children that our names were under there.

That sounded like a great idea, so we all got sticks and wrote our names and the date in the wet cement. When the steeple was actually erected, we were surprised to discover that it was not built the way we had expected. The builders left each corner of the foundation exposed. Looking at the base of the new steeple, I was shocked to see my name still showing right next to the sidewalk leading into the chapel. My friend Marshall's name was also showing on the opposite side.

How I wanted to erase that name and say I'd never written it. But there was no rubbing it out. It was there for all to see.

126

Years passed, and I became director of the seminary and institute program and Marshall became a stake president, both of us in the very area where the chapel was located. Instead of looking forward to telling our children about our names being underneath the steeple, we dreaded the day they would notice.

One day my young son came running into the meeting-house and said, "Dad, guess what! Your name is by the steeple outside. How did it get there?" What do you say? "Well, Son, sometimes youth are so outstanding that the bishop just wants to do something in their honor"? I had no choice but to tell him that I'd made a mistake and that I should have thought before I acted.

Our minds are a little bit like wet cement in the sense that whatever we inscribe there is not easily erased. The things we see, think, and hear are apparently permanently embedded in our minds. It follows that we should carefully monitor what we watch or listen to in the media, because the images we see on television or in the movies or what we listen to on the radio or stereo remain permanently filed away, subject to recall.

How influential is the media industry in our society? Several reports conclude that the media ranks third behind peers and parents in the amount of influence it has on the values and behavior of today's teens. In single-parent or dysfunctional families, movies, television, and music may have passed parents on the scale. When I was a teenager, the media ranked eighth in influence, far behind parents, peers, teachers, relatives, and religious leaders. There is no question that the entertainment media is an increasingly dominant force in our society.

Recently, our two teenaged sons were out playing

basketball in the front yard. One child in our neighborhood, a very blond, light-skinned four-year-old named Nathan, came to watch. During a pause in the action, the little boy exclaimed, "When I get big, I'm gonna be Michael Jordan! And I'm gonna be black!" No doubt our little white friend had been influenced by the powerful "be like Mike" commercials seen frequently on television. Media influence begins early, and it remains a powerful force throughout our lives.

In the early 1950s few people in our area had television sets. Our family was one of the first to purchase one. I can still remember having visitors come to our home to watch such shows as "Dennis the Menace" and "Leave It to Beaver." They were shows that depicted harmless boyhood mischief and family life within a neighborhood — all very innocent but true to life in that era. We also had an AM radio that was about five feet tall. Our family gathered around it on Friday nights and listened to innocent comedy shows. Things have changed drastically since that time. Our society is now immersed in suggestive and frequently blatant sexual programming.

Have you ever wondered how much electronic media is available to the youth of our day? The following media were found in homes and bedrooms of high school students during a recent study.

TEENAGERS' HOMES	TEENAGERS' BEDROOMS
Television 99.5%	Stereo system 91%
Stereo system 98.6%	Television 68%
VCR 91.5%	Cable television 41%
Cable television 76.5%	VCR 26%

Not only has the number of electronic media devices dramatically increased, but the amount of time spent watching or listening to them has also risen sharply. The average man, woman, or child in the United States watches twenty-eight hours of television per week. That, however, does not fully explain how much our society is actually involved with the electronic media. How much additional time is spent using radios, cassette players, and video games and going to the movies?

How about you? How much do you depend on these electronic machines for entertainment? What is the first thing you do when you wake up in the morning? The vast majority of American teenagers turn on the radio. How much do you listen to music as you drive or ride in a car? When you get home, how much time do you spend with radio, CD recordings, cassette tapes, television, music videos, video games, or movies each week? For many youth, the last ritual at night is turning off some type of electronic media. And increasing numbers leave radios and televisions playing all night. In a recent study conducted among high school teenagers, the students estimated they spend more than forty hours per week listening to and watching the electronic media.

We would all do well to ask ourselves what our own involvement with the media is. How important is it in your life? One way to think about this is to answer the following two questions:

Q. How much money would it take to get you to be away from your family for thirty days? From your Mother $____ Father $____ Brothers and Sisters $____

Q. How much money would it take to get you to give up the following electronic media for thirty days? Television $____ Movies $____ Music $____

If a large sum of money would be required to get you to

give up media and not much to be away from the members of your family, perhaps you should examine how important media entertainment is in your life.

Considering the availability of media and the time being spent with it, perhaps we all should ask ourselves, "What kind of influence is the media having on my thoughts, attitudes, and behavior?" Let's examine popular music, television, and movies somewhat more closely to more accurately determine the influence they may be having.

POPULAR MUSIC

In 1988 I was fortunate to be able to serve as the session director for Brigham Young University's "Especially for Youth" program held at Texas A&M University. It was a wonderful experience to see their lives change as the youth drew closer to Christ. Many tears were shed during the testimony meetings and at the special firesides and classes. I think everyone dreaded the thought of going back to the "real world."

The sessions ended too quickly, and I found myself beginning the long ride home on a chartered bus with members of one of the stakes from my area. Conversation on the bus centered on the spiritual feelings and experiences of these participants for about the first thirty minutes. It was a special time for me as the youth talked about sacred things.

Then one of the young men asked the bus driver to play a pop music cassette over the bus stereo system. The second song on the tape was titled, "I Want Your Sex." The song was the number one hit of that summer in many areas. It was disappointing to hear about half the youth on the bus sing along with the suggestive words to that song.

I can't fully explain what happened that day on the bus,

but I can testify that the Spirit immediately left when the song began. In fact, I didn't hear another thing mentioned about EFY the rest of the way home.

No wonder President Ezra Taft Benson has warned us not to listen to degrading music. He said, "Much of the rock music is purposely designed to push immorality" (*The Teachings of Ezra Taft Benson* [Salt Lake City: Bookcraft, 1988], p. 322). Not only can inappropriate music expel the Spirit but it can fill our minds with immoral thoughts. The time youth spend listening to rock music is alarming. Approximately 2,940 more hours are spent listening to music than are spent in school between the seventh and twelfth grades (Stewart Powell, "What Entertainers Are Doing to Our Kids," *U.S. News and World Report,* 28 Oct. 1985, pp. 46–49). Do you think it is possible to spend almost five hours a day listening to music without being affected by its content?

Music videos broadcast on MTV are currently very popular with youth and young adults between the ages of twelve and twenty. Unfortunately, many of these videos are explicitly sexual. One researcher found that 75 percent of MTV's music videos contain sexual themes. He concluded that "watching rock music videos is not passive adolescent entertainment; simply watching them can alter viewers' perceptions of the social world" (C. Hansen, "Priming Sex-Role Stereotypic Event Schemes with Rock Music Videos," *Journal of Basic and Applied Social Psychology,* Dec. 1989, pp. 373–91).

In a survey conducted by the author among 455 American high school students, an interesting correlation between music and sexual attitudes was discovered. The students were asked what kind of music they enjoyed listening to most. They were also asked to answer this question: "If you really cared about someone, would you be willing to have sexual relations with that person even though you were not married?"

Here are the percentages of young people who said they would be willing to have premarital sex, listed by their favorite type of music: classical 35 percent; soft rock 56 percent; top forty 65 percent; country 69 percent; punk rock 71 percent; rap 73 percent; alternative 80 percent; and heavy metal 84 percent. Surely music can influence those who are spending large amounts of time listening to it.

I also believe that listening to music can be addictive. If you doubt that, consider how it would affect you or your friends to go without music of any kind for seven days. This challenge has been given to thousands of teenagers, who were also asked to keep a short journal of their experience. Most will not agree to attempt it for even one day, much less seven. A small number of youth, however, do make it through the experiment. Those who do almost always go through severe withdrawal pains.

The following was written by Stacey, a nineteen-year-old LDS young woman who accepted the challenge to go three days without listening to music. Her journal entry is typical of others I have received. She wrote:

"I discovered that I am very addicted to music! The first night, on the way home from institute, I felt really strange and out of place without the radio on. I heard so many weird sounds — my tires screeching when I took off, my muffler, and all kinds of squeaks that I had never heard before. I had decided to do this, though, even if it killed me! It practically did! I concluded that I can't go to sleep without my radio. My car sounds like it's about to fall apart, and my mood and attitude change when there is no music! I seriously had to listen to meditation (ocean sounds) tapes just to go to sleep. Then the last day, I really found myself depressed.

"These past three days have been really hard for me. But I found that I studied a lot more and I talked to my parents more than I ever had. If there is such a thing as being addicted to music, then I am — 100 percent.

"P.S. Thanks for three days of torment!"

It almost sounds as if Stacey was trying to quit smoking or using drugs, instead of giving up music for three days. Music can be either a virtue or a vice, depending on the type and lyrics. Can you think of any vices that are not addicting? Whether it is gambling, tobacco, alcohol, pornography, drugs, or immorality, initial experimentation often leads to addiction. Is it any wonder that the unworthy music of our day can also be addicting?

TELEVISION

While serving as a member of a bishopric several years ago, I was often asked to give spiritual thoughts to the Primary children during sharing time. One Sunday, speaking to the younger group, I asked them to raise their hands if they knew the answer to this question: "How many of you can name the four Teenage Mutant Ninja Turtles?" Except for two very young girls, every child in the entire Primary raised his or her hand. The first four children I called on each gave me a name of one of the four turtles. I then asked a four-year-old how she knew their names. She proudly announced with a huge grin, "Because I watch them every day!"

Then I said, "Okay, kids, I have another question for you." They were visibly excited. I said, "Name one of the four sons of Mosiah in the Book of Mormon." At first they looked at me with that "what-channel-do-they-come-on" look. Then they looked at each other with blank stares. After a long silence one little girl slowly raised her hand and asked in an uncertain tone, "Is one Michelangelo?" "No," I replied. "That's a good guess, but it's not right. Can anyone else think of one?" After many confused looks, they all gave up. I then turned back to the little four-year-old girl I had begun with, and asked why she didn't know the names of the four sons of Mosiah. She was quick to answer. "Because I don't watch them every day."

Clearly, what they see on television makes strong impressions on little children. There is compelling evidence it influences older people as well — determining in many cases what we know and shaping our attitudes and perceptions. Television viewing has a profound effect in the lives of most youth, particularly those who are spending four to five hours a day in front of their sets. The typical high school graduate will have spent almost twice as much time watching television as he has spent in the classroom — the equivalent of ten years of forty-hour weeks (E.H. Methvin, "TV Violence: The Shocking New Evidence," *Reader's Digest,* Jan. 1983, pp. 49–53).

Unfortunately, television communicates the same information to everyone simultaneously, regardless of age, level of education, or experience. Young minds may have difficulty reconciling behavior portrayed in television programming with values they are being taught by parents and Church leaders. There is also a great deal of concern about the violence and brutality so often shown on television and about the effect its portrayal is having on viewers and on our society.

Producers of many television shows have turned increasingly to sexually oriented subjects and depictions that were previously considered inappropriate. For instance, a 1986 study showed that there were 176 sexual references and situations shown weekly on prime-time network television. By 1992 that number had increased to 386 implications per week. At this rate, the average teenager viewer would see more than 20,000 sexual references and situations per year. Moreover, intimate physical relations are most commonly portrayed among unmarried characters in the programming. These sexual scenes are often shown with almost no reference to the consequences of illicit sex (Stanley Greenberg, et al., "Project Cast: Sex Content on Soaps and Prime-time Television Series Most Viewed by Adolescents," Michigan, 1986). The effect of such viewing is too damaging for anyone who is concerned about morality to simply sit in front of the television, indiscriminately absorbing all the trash the machine spews out.

MOVIES

Some of the most pleasant memories of my youthful years are of attending good movies. There was no bad language, no immorality shown, and for the most part, good always triumphed in the end. Many of the movies of those days were targeted toward youth audiences.

Teenagers are still a prime target audience for moviemakers, because youth make up the majority of those buying movie tickets. Moviegoing for youth is a popular social activity, and the results of one study showed that a typical teenager watches approximately 177 movies per year.

When 1200 students were asked what kinds of movies they enjoyed viewing, 73 percent favored R-rated films, 22 percent preferred PG-13 movies, 5 percent liked PG-rated shows, and 0 percent listed G-rated movies as enjoyable. Clearly, youthful viewers disdain movies whose content is suitable for all audiences, preferring entertainment that by its rating is guaranteed to portray some measure of sex, violence, and profanity. What should also be of concern is the availability of these films to young, impressionable viewers. Theaters do little to enforce attendance guidelines, and cable television and video players are widely accessible. Many people—both youth and adults—rationalize their viewing of vulgar movies, pretending not to notice the "bad parts" or arguing that the films are otherwise so artistic or entertaining they simply must be seen. Are we being fooled? Are we being desensitized to things that are inappropriate?

I recently interviewed an eleven-year-old boy named Allen about the movies he had watched during the last year. I noted that most of the movies he named were R-rated. Knowing that his family was very active in the Church, I asked him if he'd actually seen all the movies he named. He described the details of the films in a way that convinced me he had.

I said, "Allen, who rents the movies that you watch?" He replied, "My dad and my brothers." I asked him what his mother thought about his watching these movies. "She doesn't care," he quickly replied. I then said, "Allen, tell me what good things you learned from these movies." He laughed and said that he "could not think of anything good." I told him to think harder. He finally said, "I learned how to break people's arms and necks and the other stuff." I asked him what he meant by "other stuff." He said, "You know, the sex stuff." I could hardly believe what I was hearing from one so young. He then got out of his chair and demonstrated how he could break my arms and neck. When I got him to sit down again, I asked how he felt about the prophet's counsel not to watch R-rated movies. His reply shocked me. He said, "I don't care what he says." Now I ask you, has this young

Latter-day Saint boy been affected by his exposure to inappropriate movies?

President Ezra Taft Benson has given us clear direction in this matter of entertainment. He said: "We counsel you . . . not to pollute your minds with such degrading matter, for the mind through which this filth passes is never the same afterwards. Don't see R-rated movies or vulgar videos or participate in any entertainment that is immoral, suggestive, or pornographic" (*The Teachings of Ezra Taft Benson,* p. 222).

THE THOUGHT PROCESS

One of the biggest dangers from watching movies with sexual or erotic content is that by doing so we fill our minds with carnal images and thoughts. Viewing such scenes stimulates the imagination and creates strong desires. The resulting feelings and emotions are difficult to control and often lead to transgression. A stake president recently told me that never once when he was a bishop, did any youth come to him who had sexually transgressed who had not first viewed movies with some sexual content. His observation fits well with a statement made by Elder Neal A. Maxwell: "If we entertain temptations, soon they begin entertaining us" ("Overcome . . . Even As I Also Overcame," *Ensign,* May 1987, p. 71).

It is also true that once a sexual image is introduced into our minds, it is not easily removed. Such things can be recalled through voluntary or involuntary flashbacks. Recalling the scenes renews the temptation, drives away the Spirit, and puts us in repeated danger of transgressing.

Several years ago I worked with a young woman named Teri. She loved attending movies. She frequently told me about the latest movies she had seen. I noticed that she didn't seem to care how the movies were rated. We had several discussions about the R-rated movies she was watching. I tried to teach her that they could have a negative effect on her. She tried to convince me that I was being needlessly concerned. She insisted she simply didn't "pay attention to the immoral scenes."

In time Teri received a mission call. After her release eighteen months later, she stopped by to see me. Guess what the first thing she said to me was? She said, "You were right about the R-rated movies." She went on to say that time after time, while trying to teach the discussions to investigators, images from the vulgar movies she had viewed in the past would flash into her mind. When this happened, she had to turn the teaching over to her companion, because she was unable to focus on her message. Not only do our minds have the ability to recall things we've allowed to enter them but those thoughts and images are often brought back at the most inopportune time.

President Spencer W. Kimball warned: "The body has power to rid itself of sickening food. That person who entertains filthy stories or pornographic pictures and literature records them in his marvelous human computer, the brain, which can't forget this filth. Once recorded, it will always remain there, subject to recall" (*The Teachings of Spencer W. Kimball*, ed. Edward L. Kimball [Salt Lake City: Bookcraft, 1982], p. 283).

How many times have young couples sat in darkened theaters, viewing sexual behavior portrayed to the accompaniment of beautiful music, and had their minds filled with lust? Then, stimulated by what they have viewed, how many of those same youth have succumbed to temptations before returning home? We must stop the flow of evil thoughts into our minds if we want to avoid the evil acts that follow those thoughts.

To do that, we must first realize that the thoughts themselves are sins and we will be held accountable for them. The Book of Mormon teaches that "our words will condemn us, yea, all our works will condemn us; . . . and our thoughts will also condemn us; and in this awful state we shall not dare to look up to our God" (Alma 12:14). It is important to control our thoughts because they are the seeds of our acts. Fortunately, a person has time to expel a thought when it first arises, but a thought that is not controlled can lead to transgression. Controlling thoughts is not an easy task in our sex-drenched society. In fact, for some individuals, it is one of the most difficult things they will face in mortal life. But there are ways. Let's look at some ideas for establishing personal guidelines in using electronic media.

1. Know the content

Before you attend, buy, rent, or borrow any movie, learn all you can about its content. An excellent service is called the *Entertainment Research Report.* This publication analyzes every movie that is released to the theaters and also those that come out on video. Many magazines and newspapers carry movie reviews that may also be helpful. You might talk to people who have seen the film in question. Ask specific questions: What was the language like? Any violence? Any immorality? Who are the stars? What other movies have they appeared in? Call the theater and ask the staff about the movie.

By carefully selecting the movies we view, we can increase the chance that our experiences will be uplifting and wholesome. Remember, if you still have doubts after making these inquiries, don't go!

2. Reject obscene material

Occasionally you may be exposed to inappropriate material that you did not know would be included. What will you do in that situation? We can follow Joseph's example when Potiphar's wife made advances toward him. The scripture says, "And she caught him by his garment, saying, Lie with me: and he left his garment in her hand, and fled, and got him out" (Genesis 39:12). Decide now that you will flee anything that is obscene. Most theaters will refund your money if you are offended by the material in a film. Whether the lewd material occurs in a video, in a television show, in a song, or in a book, decide now that you will turn it off or get rid of it immediately.

3. Ask, how would I feel if . . .

Before attending or during every movie or TV program you see, ask whether this is the type of movie you would feel comfortable seeing if your parents, your bishop, the prophet, or the Savior were seated beside you. If you would feel embarrassed or uncomfortable in any way, the material is not appropriate. You would be wise to choose another form of entertainment that you can feel good about.

4. Will it make a difference?

Consider whether or not it will make any difference in a few years if you see the movie. Even if everyone else you know is attending but the film contains things you know you shouldn't see, don't go. Too often we subject our minds to material that becomes part of our thoughts just because everyone else is doing it. Choose only those movies that will help make you a better person, regardless of what the critics are saying or your friends are doing.

5. Avoid that "one bad scene"

How often have you heard someone say, "It was a great movie, except for that one bad scene," or "The film has a good message, if you can get past the filthy language"? Avoid such films. Think back on a movie you may have seen that contained "just one bad scene." Can you still see that scene in your mind? If so, then any temporary pleasure or benefit you may have received from viewing it has been nullified.

6. Develop your own rating system

You need to become your own movie, music, and television critic. After determining the content of the movie or program, you can use your own criteria for rating it. You may identify as X-rated a film rated PG by the seven-member MPAA board. Keep the dictionary definition of *pornography* in mind when establishing your guidelines. The *American Heritage Dictionary* defines *pornography* as "written or pictorial matter intended to arouse sexual feelings." Can movies with so-called good ratings actually be pornographic? What about the content of some television programs or the lyrics to popular songs? The answer is yes!

7. Discuss your values with others

Another way to help protect yourself from the negative influences of inappropriate media is to openly discuss your values with friends. By letting them know where you stand on unsuitable movies, they will often quit pressuring you to participate. Word spreads just as quickly about those with high standards as it does about those with low standards. You will begin to attract people who have similar values, people you want to be around. Others may disagree with your stand, but that is okay. I have found that when a "Nephi" stands up to the pressure, a "Sam" almost always follows.

8. Use Moroni 7:13, 17 as a guide

The Book of Mormon declares "But behold, that which is of God inviteth and enticeth to do good continually; wherefore, every thing which inviteth and enticeth to do good, and to love God, and to serve him, is inspired of God. . . . But whatsoever thing persuadeth men to do evil, and believe not in Christ, and deny him, and serve not God, then ye may know with a perfect knowledge it is of the devil" (Moroni 7:13, 17).

We would do well to apply that standard to the things we watch, listen to, read, or think about.

9. Use pencil and paper to review movies and TV programs

You might want to try viewing movies and television with a pencil and paper in hand, so you can analyze the content. You will be amazed at the messages—both good and bad. In analyzing the content, use gospel principles to determine what is negative or positive. Here are some aspects to consider:

1. *Theme.* What is the purpose or the message of the movie or program? Why did the producers spend so much money to bring you this message? How would you characterize the overall message—good, bad, spiritual, immoral, silly, or patriotic?

2. *Language.* What kind of language is used? Are people respectful in communicating with one another, or do they ridicule or mock? Are off-color, vulgar jokes or dialogue included? How many profane words are used? Is the Lord's name used in vain? How many times? If you have never listened closely to the language being used in the media, you may be in for a big surprise when trying this idea.

3. *Violence.* How many acts of violence are shown? Why were they included? Are they essential to the plot?

4. *Immorality.* Were sexually related scenes shown or implied? Were there portrayals of unmarried couples living together? How were the heroes portrayed—as sexually promiscuous or virtuous? Were there any consequences shown for immorality?

5. *Other inappropriate behavior.* How much drug, tobacco, and alcohol use is shown? How are marriage and family life portrayed? What crimes were committed and were there any consequences shown?

Watching a movie or program critically and using a pencil and paper to keep counts and make notes will likely open your eyes to things you have been watching without realizing it. You will see things that you have never noticed before, and in the process build up a wall of protection, becoming more aware and eliminating from your view those films that do not meet your standards.

10. Seek Spiritual Guidance in Selecting Music

"Through music, man's ability to express himself extends beyond the limits of the spoken language in both subtlety and power. Music can be used to exalt and inspire or to carry messages of degradation and destruction. It is therefore important that as Latter-day Saints we at all times apply the principles of the gospel and seek the guidance of the Spirit in selecting the music with which we surround ourselves" (First Presidency, *Priesthood Bulletin,* Aug. 1973, as quoted in Boyd K. Packer, "Inspiring Music—Worthy Thoughts," *Ensign,* Jan. 1974, p. 25).

One stake president in an area where I lived challenged all the youth in the stake to get a basket and go through their homes. He asked them to gather up anything they would be ashamed to have the Savior see, including records, tapes,

CDs, posters, videos, magazines, and books, put them in the basket, and then dispose of them. Elder Richard L. Evans observed, "We ought to be committed to the principle of not making evil profitable" (in Conference Report, Apr. 1969, p. 74). Youth can stop the barrage of filth if they will only stand up for the right and refuse to participate.

Recently I heard a young man give a thought-provoking talk about deceit. He told a story about the devil and his helpers sitting around trying to figure out how to deceive LDS youth. One proposed the idea of telling the youth that there is *no God*. This idea was quickly rejected, the group agreeing that the youth of the Church were too well-versed in Church teachings and doctrine to be deceived by such a lie. Another suggested that they teach them there is *no devil*. That idea was also thrown out because parents of youth and the scriptures so clearly teach that the adversary is indeed real. Finally, one suggested that they teach the LDS youth that there is *no hurry*. That plan was quickly adopted.

Although this story is obviously make-believe, it illustrates an important point. I hear many of our youth say, "I'll change when I get older." The time to change is now. I challenge you to ponder your involvement with the media and quickly make any changes that may be needed.

CHAPTER 11

DATING AND
"THE SUMMER OF THE LAMBS"

JAYNE B. MALAN

The day school let out at the beginning of each summer, our family would go to our ranch in Wyoming. There, on the ranch with my parents and brothers and sisters and a few cousins mixed in, was where I learned about family loyalty, love and concern, birth and death, and that one must finish a job once it is started. I also learned — to quote my father — "There are only two things important: the family and the Church."

One year my father was waiting for us when we arrived at the ranch. He said that he had a big job for my brother, Clay, and me to do that summer. I was about twelve at the time and Clay was two years older. Pointing into the field by the side of the house, he said, "Do you see all of those lambs? I'll share the money we get for the ones you raise when we sell them in the fall." We were excited. Not only did we have a significant job to do but we were going to be rich! There were a lot of lambs in that field . . . about 350 of them. And all we had to do was feed them.

There was one thing my father hadn't mentioned, however. The lambs had no mothers. Just after shearing, a violent storm had chilled the newly shorn sheep. Dad lost a thousand ewes that year. The mothers of our orphaned lambs were among them.

To feed one or two baby animals is one thing, but to feed 350 is something else! It was hard. There was plenty of grass, but the lambs couldn't eat the grass. They didn't have teeth. They needed milk. So we made long V-shaped feeding troughs out of some boards. Then we made a thin mash by mixing ground grain and milk in a great big, tin washtub. While my brother was pouring the mash into the troughs, I rounded up the lambs, herded them to the troughs, and said, "Eat!" They just stood there looking at me. Although they were hungry and there was food in front of them, they still wouldn't eat. No one had taught them to drink mash out of a trough. So I tried pushing them toward the troughs. Do you know what happens when you try to push sheep? They run the other way. And when you lose one, you *could* lose them all because the others will follow. That is the way with sheep.

We tried lining up the lambs along the troughs and pushing their noses down into the milk, hoping they'd get a taste and want more. We tried wiggling our fingers in the milk to get them to suck on our fingers. A few of them would drink, but most of them ran away.

Many of our lambs were slowly starving to death. The only way we could be sure they were fed was to hold them in our arms, two at a time, and feed them with bottles, as you would a baby.

And then there were the coyotes. At night the coyotes would sit on the hill and howl. The next morning we would see the results of their night's work, and we would have two or three more lambs to bury. The coyotes would sneak up on the lambs and scatter the herd and then pick out the ones they wanted and go after them. The first to be killed were those that were weak or that got separated from the flock. Often in the night when the coyotes came, and the lambs were restless, Dad would take out his rifle and shoot in the air to scare the coyotes away. We felt secure when Dad was home because we knew the lambs were safe when he was there to watch over them.

Clay and I soon forgot about being rich. All we wanted to do was save our lambs. The hardest part was seeing them die. Every morning we would find five, seven, ten lambs that had died during the night. Some the coyotes got, and others starved to death, surrounded by food they couldn't or wouldn't eat.

Part of our job was to gather up the dead ones and help dispose of them. I got used to that and it wasn't so bad until I gave one of the lambs a name. It was an awkward little thing with a black spot on its nose. It was always under my feet, and it knew my voice. I loved my lamb. It was one that I had held in my arms and fed with a bottle like a baby.

One morning my lamb didn't come when I called. I found it later that day, under the willows by the creek. It was dead. With tears streaming down my face, I picked it up and went to find my father. Looking up at him, I said, "Dad, isn't there someone who can help us feed our lambs?" After a long moment he said, "Jayne, once, a long time ago, someone else said almost those same words. He said it three times. He said, 'Feed my lambs. . . . Feed my sheep. . . . Feed my sheep' " (John 21:15–17). Dad put his arms around me and let me cry for a time, and then he went with me to bury my lamb.

It wasn't until many years later that I fully realized the meaning of my father's words. I was pondering the scripture in Moses that says, "For behold, this is my work and my glory—to bring to pass the immortality and eternal life of man" (Moses 1:39). That's all mankind. As I thought about the mission of the Savior, I remembered the summer of the lambs, and, for a few brief moments, I thought I could sense how the Savior must feel with so many lambs to feed—so many souls to save. I knew in my heart he needed my help.

From what I've observed, you're not unlike our lambs. You, too, are hungry . . . hungry for things of the Spirit that will make you grow strong and keep you safe from the "coyotes" that are out to destroy you. You are capable and willing to do your part in building the kingdom when you are taught how.

You need someone to love you, someone to listen to and understand you. You need to be needed. You need opportunities to come together in a safe environment, a safe fold, so to speak, where you can share with one another and develop wholesome friendships based on brother-sister relationships rather than romantic involvement, which should come later. You need opportunities to experience the joy of sacrifice and service, of caring for and loving one another in the same way the Savior loves us.

Within the gospel we have what you need, but you need to reach out and accept it. The Savior wants you to be happy while you are fulfilling your mission here on earth. Such happiness comes from knowing and living the gospel. He wants you to prepare to return to him, with honor, when the time comes. Now is the time for preparation.

You may ask, "But how does all of this relate to dating?"

During the dating years and in dating situations many of your needs can be filled. This is also the time when you will be making important decisions that will influence your life forever. They involve choices—choices in regard to friends, education, career, mission, marriage, parenthood—the things that will influence the kind of person you will become. This is a time of testing to see who you will choose to follow and who will follow you.

The years when you are dating can be the most rewarding or the most destructive of your entire lifetime. It will all depend on where you go, what you do, and with whom. This is a critical time for you when hormones are racing, feelings are intense, and relationships are tenuous. It is the time of your life when you are most vulnerable to the powers of Satan. He knows the hearts and minds of young people, and, like the coyotes, he'll sneak up on you when you're the weakest. He would have you for his own. You must not let that happen. It's so sad to lose a lamb.

GUIDELINES FOR DATING

A cedar post and wire fence surrounded the field where Clay and I kept our lambs. Every day or so we'd check the fence to see that there weren't any holes in it and that it was secure enough to keep the lambs from wandering away and getting lost.

The guidelines for dating can be likened to the fence around our field of lambs. They suggest appropriate behavior that will help keep you safe during the years when you are forming important relationships. The guidelines have been adapted from the booklet on standards prepared under the direction of the First Presidency entitled *For the Strength of Youth.*

I hope you will view these dating guidelines as a protection and a guide for you, not as a fence to lock you in. They identify safe boundaries and have been written to help you have fun and enjoy the dating years to the fullest. They could also be compared to the food we prepared for our lambs. The food would have helped more lambs survive, but many of them wouldn't eat. If you will accept Heavenly Father's standards, you will be in a better position to govern yourself, make the right choices, and avoid the disastrous consequences of poor decisions.

Guideline 1: Begin now to prepare for a temple marriage

Dating guidelines have been established by the Church to help you prepare for temple marriage. Proper dating will help protect you and keep the "coyotes" away that are out to destroy you as you progress toward that goal.

No hard and fast rules can answer all of your questions about proper dating because everyone's needs are different. Proper dating depends on how old you are, what your cultural background may be, what opportunities for dating are available to you, what your relationship is with your parents and how they may feel about your dating, what your experience with dating has been, and especially, what your future goals may be.

I've often been asked, "What's a date?" A date is sometimes described as the sharing of a planned experience or event by two people of the opposite sex. Dating has also been defined as "a social engagement of two young people with no commitment beyond the expectation that it will be a pleasurable event for both" (Ernest Watson Burgess and Harvey J. Locke, *The Family: From Institution to Companionship* [New York: American Book Co., 1953], p. 331).

In some cultures there's no dating at all. Marriages are arranged by parents or another intermediary, and the pairing off of young men and young women before marriage is not acceptable behavior. In other areas, where dating is allowed, a chaperon must go along.

In American culture, dating is a well-accepted fact of life. It provides a way to become acquainted with members of the opposite sex and to learn the social skills that are essential in the relationship between husbands and wives. It would be a tragedy if unwholesome activities or inappropriate behavior were to intrude into your dating experience, particularly if those things should prevent you from eventually marrying in the temple.

Guideline 2: In cultures where dating is appropriate, do not date until you are sixteen years old

President Spencer W. Kimball advised us not to date before the age of sixteen. The counsel of the Church has not changed since he said: "When you get in the teen-age years, your social associations should still be general acquaintance with both boys and girls. Any dating or pairing off in social contacts should be postponed until at least the age of sixteen or older, and even then there should be much judgment used in selections and in the seriousness" ("The Marriage Decision," *Ensign*, Feb. 1975, p. 4).

The years before you begin dating are years of self-discovery. They could be described as the "wonder" years. You wonder who you are and what you're supposed to do and why. You wonder if the time will ever pass until you're sixteen and can date. If you're older than sixteen and not yet dating, you wonder if you ever will.

Avoid getting overanxious about dating. You're here on earth to be tested. Many young people aren't ready to date during their teen years and others simply need more time before forming serious relationships. A recent survey showed that more than half the young women who graduated from high school had never had a date. You don't need to date to build memories and have fun.

Take advantage of this time in your life to develop the qualities in yourself that you hope eventually to find in those you date. Those qualities might include honesty, patience, kindness, understanding, and courage to stand firm in the face of negative peer pressure. It's your time to grow phys-ically, mentally, socially, and spiritually. This is the time to study hard in school and to learn more about the gospel along with ways to live and share it. It's the time to take advantage of every opportunity that comes along to develop your talents and make friends—lots of friends. Friends who are young men. Friends who are young women.

The best way to make friends and get acquainted is to do a variety of fun and worthwhile things together before you begin dating. Work together in quorum and class presidencies and on projects and in committees at church and school. Team sports and individual sports such as tennis, golf, and swimming are particularly good to help you get acquainted. Participate in roadshows, drama, music, dancing. Find ways to be of service to others. As you share experiences such as those, you'll learn from each other and grow socially. You'll learn to understand and to respect each other's differences. You'll discover that men and women are different, even at this age. They have different interests and different talents, and they don't react the same or think the same. It has always been so. An understanding of this fact will be helpful when you begin to date.

If you are under the age of sixteen and wondering whether to accept a date or not, it is a real test, especially if all of your friends, both members and nonmembers, are accepting dates. Joseph Smith said it was his practice to teach correct principles and let the people govern themselves. You were born with your agency, and you're free to choose whether to date or not. There's no law against it, only the counsel of the prophets.

Do you believe what the prophets teach? Are you willing to abide by their counsel? Or do you think this is an example of one place they are out of touch with reality? "After all," you may rationalize, "I'm almost sixteen and it's only a date. What difference will it make?" In part, this issue is a matter of obedience and trusting the Lord. I'm impressed with how many young people, all over the Church, are choosing to obey this counsel and discovering the rewards of waiting. As one young woman put it, "When you start dating too soon, it's like opening all of your presents before Christmas. I'm glad I waited."

Youth who learn to be obedient master a principle that will be a continuing source of strength in their lives.

There's nothing magic about the number sixteen. Research has shown, however, that age sixteen seems to indicate a level of maturity that makes young people more responsible for their actions. They are more likely to have long-range goals and to think before they act. As a result, fewer unwed pregnancies occur among young people who wait until age sixteen to begin dating than occur among those who begin dating before that time.

Even one unwed pregnancy is too many. It could be possible to eliminate this unhappy circumstance among Church members, along with the heartache and suffering it brings, if young people would discipline themselves on their dates and adhere to this and the other guidelines established by our prophet for proper dating.

Guideline 3: When you begin dating, go in groups or on double dates

Avoid pairing off exclusively with one partner. It's all right to be nervous about first dates. Everyone is, especially if you don't know the person you're dating very well. It's a matter of wanting to do things right and desiring to be accepted as someone of worth when you don't really know what's expected. I noticed that my son was even more nervous than my daughter when he first started dating. It takes time to learn the "rules" of successful dating. It takes time to get acquainted with yourself and to determine how you're going to react to unfamiliar feelings and circumstances.

It is good counsel to go in a group when you're beginning to date and later on as well. If there is just you and your date, then you are really on the spot to keep the conversation going. In a larger group, others can fill in the quiet spots and their personalities can be depended on to keep things going and interesting. Group activities allow you to observe a variety of people and learn from each of them. Then, too, you are not left alone with someone who might put pressure on you to do things you know are not right.

There are a number of things you need to know about dating. One is that you do not have to feel obligated to "pay" for your date by becoming intimate in return for favors or generous treatment. Invitations to compromise your standards need not be tolerated. You would do well to remember that dating is "a social engagement . . . *with no commitment beyond the expectation that it will be a pleasurable event for both."* The only thing that you "owe" your date is to be congenial and courteous. And that does *not* include granting sexual favors. If your date demands behavior of you that you are not comfortable with, then you know you have a "coyote" on your trail and you'd better get out of there, *FAST!* Don't think twice. *JUST GO!* And then don't let there be a "next time." Stay away from people, places, and situations that could cause this to happen again! It isn't worth the risk.

If a mission is part of future plans for either you or your date, you need to be extra careful. Limit your dating to groups or go with another couple and *DON'T PAIR OFF!* There is nothing "coyotes" like better than preying on future missionaries. Obeying this guideline will help you and your date stay within the boundaries of proper dating and postpone making lasting commitments until after the mission is successfully completed. Then is the time for more serious dating that can lead to temple marriage and an eternal relationship.

Going steady indicates a level of commitment to each other that often excludes association with others and limits friendships. Ardeth Kapp, the former Young Women general president, had this to say about steady dating: "It increases the risk of developing intimacy, which threatens your obedience to the commandments and your loyalty to eternal covenants, and it imposes temptations, which Satan uses to get [young] people under his influence and rob them of the blessings that come through obedience" (*The Fight for Right: Strength for Youth in the Latter Days* [Salt Lake City: Deseret Book, 1992], p. 10).

The proper time for going steady is when you're ready to get married and you are in the process of selecting your eternal companion. Even then, you need to be watchful. It's doubtful that you'll have your father along with his rifle to keep you safe. If the time comes—and it will come if you follow the natural tendencies of most young people in love—when you're alone and it's dark and things seem to be getting out of hand, you could always whisper, "I think I heard a coyote." And by the time you have explained to your date all about coyotes and how they destroy helpless lambs, the moment of danger will have passed and you can be in control again. Don't let down your guard for a minute.

While you are searching for that perfect mate, going steady can be helpful. When you have an increased level of commitment, you will most likely find more time to be together and become acquainted with your date's strengths and weaknesses. At the same time, you will be determining how well your personalities blend. That is important before marriage. But you'll never really get acquainted if all you do is go to movies or watch television together. You need variety in your dating.

In our family, we found that taking our dates to the ranch for a weekend was a wonderful way of seeing how much we liked each other and how compatible we were. It gave us an opportunity to be with our dates over an extended period of time in a chaperoned setting where we could see how they reacted to a wide variety of situations and circumstances. Those who passed the "test," we continued to date. As for the others, the trip was worthwhile, but too long for everyone. And that was the end of that.

Not everyone has a ranch to go to, but anyone can plan creative dates. We'll talk about that under Guideline 4. The important thing is to find ways to discover what you need to know about each other. One way would be to take a group of disabled children to the park. Think of all the things you could learn about each other from that experience.

You may find that you will go steady with several different dates before you finally know which one is right for you. Don't be in a hurry. Eternity is a long time. It's a date that never ends.

Some do end, however. I keep thinking about the lambs we tried to raise without their mothers. It would have been so much easier if their mothers had been there. Likewise, I think of children who are being raised by single parents because of divorce. Please take your time in selecting your marriage partner. Date long enough — associate with each other long enough — to become good friends before you become husband and wife and mother and father. Then, maybe, just maybe, this terrible trend of "falling out of love" can be reversed and there won't be so many broken homes in which children are being raised by single parents.

Guideline 4: Plan positive and constructive activities to do when you are together

Do things that will reveal the various facets of your personalities. People behave quite differently in church than they might at a water park or while eating in a fine restaurant. Take care also to go places where there is a good environment and avoid settings where you might be confronted with temptations.

The kinds of positive and constructive things you can do that will help you get to know each other better are limited only by your imagination. By using a creative approach to dating, you can have fun wherever you are — at home, at church, around your neighborhood, in your city, or out in nature. The setting doesn't matter nearly as much as having the right people there to share it with you.

A special friend of mine once said, "Fun is an attitude, not an event." That is true. If you go someplace thinking you're going to have fun, you will. You'll look for the happy things and the funny things that are happening and ignore the rest. Try it.

One of the best ideas for adding variety to your dates is to go with groups of friends that include both young men and young women. That eliminates the need to be anyone's specific girlfriend or boyfriend, and everyone can relax and have fun. You can enlarge your circle of friends in this way and broaden your experience. It's a lot more fun when four, six, or eight of you do things together. Why not five, seven, or nine? Then you can include others who don't usually date. There's no rule that says you must go two by two. The people in the groups that I dated with when I was in college are the ones who have become my lifelong friends. We cared about each other and loved each other. Some of us even married each other. This was my "safe fold." You can create your own.

The next time you're wondering what to do on a date, use the Creative Dating Chart shown on page 159 and design your own personalized list of possible dates. All you have to do is gather your favorite people together and challenge them to come up with some ideas. Then fill in the blanks. Some ideas may be *too* creative, but write them down anyway. You don't have to use them. When this chart is full, get another piece of paper and keep thinking.

Guideline 5: Date only those who share your values and respect your standards

Don't compromise your determination to be prepared for a temple marriage and the opportunity to raise your children in the Church. You don't want to take the chance of not being worthy to receive the promised blessings of glory, immortality, and eternal life that are available to you in the temple of the Lord. Therefore, date only those people who have high standards, respect your standards, and in whose

CREATIVE DATING CHART

EXPECTATION FOR THE DATE	DATING IDEAS
Get acquainted	Share favorite scriptures Play board games _____ _____ _____
Become friends	Have a picnic and take a long walk Serve on a committee _____ _____ _____
Gain knowledge	Learn about stars Visit a museum _____ _____ _____
Develop talents	Write a script and produce a video Study together _____ _____ _____
Give service	Take young family members to the zoo Prepare a meal and take it to a shut-in Do baptisms for the dead _____ _____ _____
Build testimony	Choose a scriptural theme and have a discussion Attend a fireside Visit the temple grounds _____ _____ _____

company you can maintain the standards of the gospel of Jesus Christ. Your Heavenly Father knows you and cares about what you are doing. You have a vital role to fill in his eternal plan. You have been chosen by the Lord to come to earth at this time to fulfill your special mission and assist the Savior with his work here on earth — to help feed his lambs.

Reach out to those around you. Encourage them. Support them in making wise choices, especially when decisions are difficult and may not be popular with the group. Reach out to your nonmember friends and involve them in your positive and constructive activities. Let them see the gospel in action and in *your* actions wherever you go, whatever you do.

Make dating a wholesome, happy activity in your life. Rally your friends around you. Band together in the strength of the Lord and lead out in righteousness. Reach out with loving arms and understanding hearts to those who are weak or wandering. Help bring them back to the fold where they can learn of the Good Shepherd and grow close to him.

Please choose carefully the paths you walk, for others will follow. That is the way with sheep. Of our little flock we saved only one third. And what of the Savior's flock? He has said, "Feed my lambs. . . . Feed my sheep."

CHAPTER 12

RESISTING TEMPTATION
IN AN IMMORAL WORLD

RICHARD PETERSON

We live in a world that is preoccupied with sex. Nearly every national magazine aimed at teenaged or young adult readers has a regular feature on sexuality. Written without regard to the marital status of readers, advice is given on the most intimate subjects — masturbation, contraception, and intercourse. The assumption is that even young teens are interested in and need this kind of information.

Look at advertising strategies. Whether it's automobiles, clothing, perfume, liquor, tobacco products, tools, vacation spots, airline travel, sports equipment, grooming aids, luggage, or even food products, it is a rare advertisement that doesn't use sex or sex appeal to attract the attention of the potential buyer.

Popular music, movies, fiction, videos, and television shows are also frequently filled with sexual innuendos, descriptions, or portrayals.

Comedians and entertainers frequently make reference to sexual subject matter, often in coarse and vulgar terms — in their albums, in their public performances, and on television.

Of this trend, Elder Boyd K. Packer has said: "The rapid, sweeping deterioration of values is characterized by a preoccupation—even an obsession—with the procreative act. Abstinence before marriage and fidelity within it are openly scoffed at—marriage and parenthood ridiculed as burdensome, unnecessary. Modesty, a virtue of a refined individual or society is all but gone. . . . That which should be absolutely private is disrobed and acted out center stage" ("Our Moral Environment," *Ensign*, May 1992, p. 66).

And all this is true without mentioning anything about the increased availability of pornography and all the sexual perversions it promotes.

This is the moral environment in which you are growing up. The question is, how is it possible for you to withstand the pressures being exerted on you? What can you do to successfully live the law of chastity given to us by the Lord and taught by his Church?

THE CHALLENGE

As you grew into adolescence there developed in you the physical ability to procreate life. If you are a young woman, you became capable of getting pregnant. If you are a young man, you developed the ability to father children. With this development there also came an awakening of the desire to express those powers. You began to take an increased interest in members of the opposite sex.

What you must not lose sight of is the guideline the Lord has established for the use of these sacred powers. He has expressly forbidden any of us to have sexual intercourse, except with the partner to whom we are legally married. If you are single, you have no license to express your sexuality—either with someone of your own sex, the opposite sex, or by yourself. That means no masturbation, fondling, petting, or oral sex.

Violations of the law of chastity are sinful. In fact, the Lord has instructed us that the commission of sexual sins, such as fornication and adultery, is such a serious matter that it can have eternal consequences.

Your challenge is to keep yourself sexually pure in an environment where mistaken, uninformed, or evil people will attempt to convince you that there is no sin in any of this and that the expression of your sexuality is natural and of no consequence.

HOW CAN YOU AVOID SEXUAL TRANSGRESSION?

The most obvious way to avoid sexual transgression is to develop appropriate relationships with members of the opposite sex. Our Church leaders have consistently taught that there is danger in early dating, and they have told us that we should not date until we are sixteen or older. But it should also be noted that many young people lose their virtue before they ever have a traditional date.

There is danger in such seemingly innocent activities as playing together in neighborhoods after dark or in spending time together alone in unsupervised settings—in such places as someone's house after school before parents arrive home in the evening. Whenever or wherever young people are together in social settings, there is danger unless you take care to treat your boyfriends or girlfriends with respect and resolve not to experiment on any level with forbidden activities.

When you are old enough to arrange or accept dates, you must take care that you don't put yourself in situations where you may be overcome by temptation. One of the best safeguards is to refrain from single dating. By going with other couples or in groups, you will not likely be left alone with your date or get into a situation where physical intimacies can take place.

Here is another consideration. Each of us is naturally inhibited in our first experiences with members of the opposite sex. That is why it is so terribly awkward the first time you go out with a date to eat, or to a dance, or even on a walk. By spending time together, you probably begin to feel less awkward and become more sure of yourself. Gaining confidence makes dating more fun, but spending too much time together promotes familiarity and can eventually entirely erode the inhibitions. That is why you have been counseled against "going steady" or spending too much time with any one date. As a safeguard against too much intimacy, some young people decline consecutive dates with the same person.

Older young adults, those who have perhaps dated a great deal and who might even have become engaged, must take special care to ensure their commitment to marry isn't used to justify inappropriate intimacy. The engagement does not provide any additional license for sexual expression. Great care must be taken at this point in a relationship to control expressions of affection. Some engaged couples put their bishop and stake president in a very difficult position when they come for their temple recommend interviews after having been guilty of heavy petting or fornication. They act unfairly in expecting the priesthood leader to issue them a recommend so they won't be embarrassed by having to cancel their plans for a temple marriage.

SOME SPECIFIC WARNINGS

1. *Single dating.* Being alone together too much breeds familiarity and invites inappropriate intimacy. If you are

serious about keeping your standards, you will do well to double date or to go to events and activities in groups.

2. *Modesty.* When you hear the word *modesty,* perhaps you think immediately of clothing. Certainly the kind of clothing you wear is critical. Skimpy or tight, revealing clothes make a certain statement about how you perceive yourself, and if you choose to dress provocatively, you run the risk of sending a message you may not intend. But there is more to modesty than the clothes you wear. Your speech, body language, and behavior should also reflect your values. All of these things are observed by others, and they make judgments about you based on what they see. By dressing conservatively, you will do much to minimize temptations.

3. *Fatigue.* Fatigue lowers resistance to temptation. Even if you have made a strong commitment to keep yourself morally clean, spending time together after you are tired can be dangerous. Setting a curfew with each other and with your parents establishes a target time to be safely home. After the dance is over, the show has let out, and the restaurant is closed, the things that remain to be done may lead to temptation and trouble.

4. *Reclining together.* Some couples get in the habit of lying down together to watch television. Some think they can even wrap up together in a quilt without putting themselves in jeopardy. Lying in each other's arms for long periods of time is an unwise activity for those who wish to resist temptation.

5. *Dancing.* Modern dances are generally fun and require a great deal of energy. Many of today's youth have not learned any dance steps to use when slow music is played. By default they often fall into a full-body embrace sometimes called the "bearhug" and simply sway to the music. This intimate and

stimulating way to dance has the potential to inflame the emotions.

6. *Alcohol and drugs*. Under the influence of alcohol and drugs, standards and resolve become fuzzy. Natural inhibitions are lowered, and good judgment is set aside. Many young people have lost their virtue while intoxicated or high. Some have not even been aware of what they have done — which doesn't, however, absolve anyone of guilt. Obedience to the Word of Wisdom is a powerful help in resisting temptation.

7. *Automobiles*. The use of a car usually makes dating more fun. When you are able to drive, you don't have to depend on parents for transportation. But cars also provide the opportunity to seek out isolated locations. Seated together in a car in a remote place, late at night, a couple is probably in as great a danger of losing their virtue as in any other place they could be. "Making out" is a dangerous activity. It stimulates the passions and frequently leads to immorality. Avoid parking as a recreational activity.

8. *Movies and videos*. Much of the content of movies and videos these days is frankly erotic. Viewing such films stimulates the imagination and arouses the passions. It is a lie to insist that you can watch portrayals of passionate behavior without becoming stimulated to some extent. A great deal of immoral behavior and the loss of virtue can be traced directly to the effect had on young couples by the movies they have watched.

9. *Pornography*. What is true of many movies and videos is equally true of pornographic magazines, books, and films. Viewing such material stimulates sexual desire, erodes the determination to remain virtuous, distorts the viewer's standards, and lowers resistance to immoral behavior.

SOME STRATEGIES TO HELP YOU SUCCEED

1. *Defend yourself.* Many young people are made uneasy by the behavior of their friends or dates. A date who insists on public (or private) displays of affection can be a pain. So can a date who attempts to touch you inappropriately. The best way to put an end to that kind of behavior is to emphatically tell him or her to stop it, and then insist on it. To avoid kissing, turn your head away. Sometimes saying something humorous will defuse the situation. The point is, you don't need to submit to any kind of treatment or behavior that offends you or makes you feel uneasy.

2. *Respect yourself.* Think of your virtue as a treasured possession. Don't permit anyone to trifle with your emotions or tamper with your body or chastity. Consider how your behavior would look to the Lord, to your parents, or to other people you love and admire, if they were to observe you in some compromising situation.

3. *Think about your future spouse.* Would you be happy knowing your future spouse had been sexually intimate with someone or several others prior to your marriage? Resolve to take your virtue to your marriage as a gift and then work to preserve it for that purpose.

4. *Don't rationalize.* Significant events such as senior high school trips, state championship celebrations, and graduation activities sometimes provide opportunities to escape parental supervision or to be with friends while you are in a festive mood. Take care on such occasions not to lower your standards or to give way to a mood of carelessness. When the celebration is over, you will still have to live with yourself and the consequences of your actions.

5. *Use your imagination.* If you are tempted to be immoral, try to imagine what it would be like to have to inform your

parents or your date's parents that you have disqualified yourselves for a temple marriage or that there is a pregnancy to deal with. Or think what it would be like to have to confess your immoral behavior to your bishop or to have your brothers or sisters or a respected leader learn of it — a seminary teacher, priesthood adviser, or Young Women adviser. Can you picture the kind of humiliation you might experience?

6. *Stay active in the Church*. Attend your meetings. Go to seminary. Participate in your priesthood, Young Women, or Scouting activities. Partake of the sacrament and think about your covenants. Go to your interviews when you are invited by your leaders. Be truthful and open with them.

7. *Personal strength*. Say your prayers. Read the scriptures. Obtain and then regularly review your patriarchal blessing. Live to be worthy of the influence of the Holy Ghost. Ask for a priesthood or a father's blessing. Use good judgment in choosing who you date, where you go, and what you do.

8. *Think about your future children*. What is the legacy you want to give them? Imagine the love you will have for them and the kind of trust you will want them to have in you. If you have been immoral in your youth, how difficult will it be to try to teach them about morality?

THE PITFALLS OF STEADY DATING

I once knew a wonderful young woman I'll call Candice. During her high school years, she was attractive and lively and had many friends and admirers, but in spite of her popularity, she was insecure and often moody. She spent a lot of time evaluating her appearance, worrying about her complexion, wishing she were taller and her figure more willowy.

Candice attended school with a young man I'll call Brad. He was a year ahead of her in school. Brad was also popular —

a good athlete and handsome — and he had what everybody in their school agreed was a hot car. But Brad was also more insecure than anyone might have suspected. He needed the constant reinforcement he received through playing on the school teams. He kept his car immaculately clean and highly polished. He liked it when people looked at him admiringly or praised him for playing a good game.

Candice and Brad started to date regularly after he invited her to the homecoming dance in the fall when she was a junior and he was a senior. From that point on, neither of them had any interest in dating anyone else. Besides, everyone at school knew they were "going together," and so no one ever thought to ask either of them for a date.

One reason they went together so much was that they found they had a lot in common. The night of their first date, they admitted to each other that they were not as happy as their friends assumed. Brad's parents were divorced, and even though his dad gave him money and attended all his games, Brad was confused about his parents' relationship and hated the tension he felt whenever his mom and dad were together. Candice told Brad how much she wished she looked different and how she was always worrying about what her friends might be saying about her behind her back. They admitted things to each other during that first date together that they had never shared with anybody else. They both enjoyed the date immensely, and by the time they said goodnight on her doorstep, they were starting to fall in love.

It was only natural they would want to be together again and often. And so began a relationship that intensified during that school year. At first they were content just to be together — between classes, after games, at the movies, at school dances, at the library, and at lunch. Candice's parents liked

Brad because he was always polite, and Brad's mother thought Candice was "just a doll." Both sets of parents were pleased their children had found such an impressive friend, and they were allowed to date pretty much whenever and however they wished.

The trouble started sometime following Christmas. After going to a movie in which there was a provocative love scene, Brad drove to a secluded lookout on the hills above the city. They sat for a time, looking at the lights and talking. They held hands and then began to kiss. This wasn't the first time they had done so, but stimulated by what they had watched together in the theater, they both surrendered to their desires. Ignoring their feelings that what they were doing was wrong, they permitted their hands to wander and were soon locked in a passionate embrace neither of them had the willpower to break.

You can finish the story. You can perhaps imagine how Brad and Candice must have felt later that night, as each went home and then lay in bed agonizing over the mistake they had made. Maybe you can put yourself in their shoes some time later as they told their parents that Candice was pregnant, or as they went to their bishop to confess their transgression, to pour out their sorrow, and to begin the difficult process of repentance. Maybe you can imagine how it was for them at school when news of their hastily arranged marriage circulated through the halls and in the cafeteria. Perhaps you can feel how Brad felt when he realized there would be no mission call for him. Or you might think about how Candice felt about giving up her senior year in high school to have and then care for their baby.

CONCLUSION

Teenagers and young adults who get into this kind of trouble usually don't plan to do so. But, caught in the powerful currents of their youthful passions, they can be swept along, helpless to control where the flow takes them. The only safety is not to venture out into the river.

As you read this, think about what the Lord has told us about morality. Think about the consequences of disobedience. Perhaps more importantly, consider the happiness that you will experience if you keep yourself morally clean, if you are worthy of a temple recommend, and if you can go to your marriage knowing that you are pure and virtuous. Resisting temptation and keeping the commandment to be morally clean really is worth it.

CHAPTER 13

THE BLESSINGS OF REPENTANCE
AND THE REWARDS
FOR RIGHTEOUSNESS

BRENT L. TOP

Though your sins be as scarlet, they shall be white as snow;
though they be red like crimson, they shall be as wool.
Isaiah 1:18

A few years ago my wife and I had the opportunity to travel in the Middle East for several weeks. During our visit to Egypt, we experienced some feelings that we will never forget. It was there that we had our first encounter with the conditions of poverty and uncleanliness that prevail in so many of the underdeveloped countries of the world. Our accommodations did not include the conveniences of sanitation and privacy to which we were accustomed. Complicating these conditions was the extraordinary heat of an unusually hot and dry Egyptian summer. We were exposed to intense heat as we visited the tombs and temples of the ancient pharaohs. The physical exertion and strain of walking the dusty paths in the almost unbearable desert heat soon left us sweaty, stinky, grimy, grouchy, and exhausted. At the end of a visit to any particular site, there was often a hurried retreat to the oasis-like comfort of our air-conditioned tour buses. All too often, however, the buses overheated and the air-conditioning failed.

After one particularly long day of this "touring torture," during which we had no chance to bathe or change clothes, we boarded a late-night train for a return trip to Cairo. We were cramped in hot and stuffy sleeping quarters in the old Luxor train, which seemed to have square wheels as it bumped and bounced along. It was futile to attempt to sleep during the fourteen-hour trip. The unpleasant odor of the dirty and sweaty travelers commingled with the stench coming from the primitive sanitation facilities, adding queasiness to our discomfort. Oh, how we longed to return to the comforts of our four-star hotel in Cairo.

I can't remember ever feeling so dirty, so fatigued, and so uncomfortable. I did not want to go another mile, see another ancient site, or learn another important historical fact. I knew that I might never be able to visit these places again, yet all I cared about was getting back to the hotel. I just wanted to be clean! It seemed like the longest day of my life as I counted the hours, minutes, and even the seconds until the bus finally arrived at our hotel.

Never before had a shower, a shampoo, and a shave felt so exquisite. It felt so good finally to be clean again. It felt so good to be able to rest. It felt so good to be, in a small way, at peace.

That experience of being physically dirty in Egypt has helped me understand something Isaiah said about the spiritual side effects of sin: "But the wicked are like the troubled sea, when it cannot rest, whose waters cast up mire and dirt. There is no peace, saith my God, to the wicked" (Isaiah 57:20–21).

Perhaps only a few of us have had an experience similar to this one, but *all* of us have had encounters with the uncomfortable consequences of sin. The preacher in Ecclesiastes declared, "For there is not a just man upon the earth, that doeth good, and sinneth not" (Ecclesiastes 7:20). The apostle Paul reminds us that "all have sinned, and come short of the glory of God" (Romans 3:23). Each of us has indeed sinned, and though the nature of our sins and the burdens of guilt may vary, we all know well the spiritual discomfort that accompanies our iniquities. Who among us has not experienced feelings, to a greater or lesser degree, like those described in the Book of Mormon by Alma? "But I was racked with eternal torment, for my soul was harrowed up to the greatest degree and racked with all my sins.

"Yea, I did remember all my sins and iniquities, for which I was tormented with the pains of hell; yea, I saw that I had rebelled against my God, and that I had not kept his holy commandments.

". . . yea, and in fine so great had been my iniquities, that the very thought of coming into the presence of my God did rack my soul with inexpressible horror.

"Oh, thought I, that I could be banished and become extinct both soul and body, that I might not be brought to stand in the presence of my God, to be judged of my deeds.

". . . I [was] racked, even with the pains of a damned soul" (Alma 36:12–16).

Each of us could describe just such painful emotions resulting from our own disobedience. We have learned through personal experience that sin destroys our self-esteem, damages our faith, and can lead to hopelessness and despair. The burden of sin creates a feeling of worthlessness as well as unworthiness. Thus, when we are weighted down with the

burdens of sin, our souls are truly like the river of filthy waters
which Nephi saw in vision (see 1 Nephi 15:26–30), made
turbulent by the constant churning of guilt and shame.

Satan would love to keep us in this miserable state forever.
He wants us to feel that we cannot possibly be loved by our
Heavenly Father or Jesus Christ after we have defiled ourselves with worldly ways. The father of lies is delighted when
we convince ourselves that it is impossible for us to be completely forgiven and cleansed from the stains of sin. He knows
that the feelings of being unlovable and unforgivable are
towering roadblocks to repentance. They cause us to be tormented with doubts about ourselves and our Savior. "What
if this burden of sin and shame can never be lifted?" and
"What if I must feel 'eternal torment' and the 'pains of hell'
forever?" Surely these thoughts strike within us the feeling
described by Alma as "inexpressible horror."

In fact, these "what ifs" would have become reality except
for the loving intercession of our Savior, Jesus Christ. Without
his "infinite atonement," not only would we have been left
to suffer the pains of hell but we would have continued to
carry the burdens of the sin we acquired in mortality. Lacking
the power to rid ourselves of the effects of sin, "our spirits
must have become like unto him [the devil], and we become
devils, angels to a devil, to be shut out from the presence of
our God, and to remain with the father of lies, in misery" (2
Nephi 9:7, 9). Because of their eternal and incomprehensible
love for us, our Heavenly Father and his Beloved Son have
prepared "a way for our escape from the grasp of this awful
monster; yea, that monster, death and hell" (2 Nephi 9:10).
Troubled souls can be soothed and calmed. The stains of sin
can be removed. Hope can replace despair, and the tears of
sinful sorrow can be wiped from our faces. Joy can swallow

up guilt. "Though your sins be as scarlet, they shall be as white as snow; though they be red like crimson, they shall be as wool" (Isaiah 1:18). That is the great hope we have in Jesus Christ.

Thus, we must not fall prey to Lucifer's lies. No matter who you are, no matter how low and unworthy you may feel, you are not rejected, nor alone, nor forgotten—God loves you still. Elder Richard G. Scott of the Quorum of the Twelve Apostles, testified of God's love and the Savior's atonement and counseled us to pray for the spiritual strength required for our repentance:

"I cannot comprehend [God's] power, his majesty, his perfections. But I do understand something of his love, his compassion, his mercy.

"There is no burden he cannot lift.

"There is no heart he cannot purify and fill with joy.

"There is no life he cannot cleanse and restore when one is obedient to his teachings....

"He is your Father; pray to him. If your life is in disarray and you feel uncomfortable and unworthy to pray because you are not clean, don't worry. He already knows about all of that. He is waiting for you to kneel in humility and take the first few steps. Pray for strength. Pray for others to be led to support you and guide you and lift you. Pray that the love of the Savior will pour into your heart. Pray that the miracle of the Atonement will bring forgiveness because you are willing to change. I know that those prayers will be answered, for God loves you. His Son gave his life for you. I know they will help you" ("True Friends That Lift," *Ensign,* Nov. 1988, p. 77).

REPENTANCE IS NOT A "CHECKLIST"

As Elder Scott so kindly pointed out, God is patiently waiting for us to take the first few steps. Sometimes, though, we make of repentance only a series of steps to be taken or items on a checklist to be completed for each sin that we may commit. We may teach these steps as the "Rs of Repentance" or some other catchy name. Such a checklist approach may serve as a memory device or a teaching method, but it does not accurately or completely teach the true nature and doctrine of repentance. It tends to leave out the most important ingredient of all—faith in the Lord Jesus Christ.

Although the familiar "Rs" or other similar approaches to repentance are good and important actions, they will not produce a remission of sins without the good motive, the real and righteous intent that springs from true faith in Christ. Moreover, a preoccupation with outward performances may overshadow the inward "workings of the Spirit" that will ultimately result in a thorough change of life. Perhaps the following true stories will best illustrate some of the problems with "checklist repentance."

A young woman approached the bishop of her ward minutes before sacrament meeting. "I need to talk with you," she told the bishop. The bishop looked at his watch and offered to make an appointment with her after the meeting. She insisted that what she needed to say would only take a moment.

"Last night I committed fornication," she announced to the bishop. "I am here to confess that transgression to you, since I know that confession is one of the steps of repentance."

The bishop explained that they would need to meet together right after sacrament meeting to discuss the matter

further, resolve problems, and talk about the true meaning
of repentance. She resisted and responded that she could not
understand why an additional interview would be necessary
since she had already *recognized* her sin, felt *remorse, confessed*
to the bishop, and *resolved* that the sinful act would not happen again. In her mind she had completed all of the "steps
of repentance" that she had been taught. Yet, she demonstrated little understanding of the central role of faith in
Christ and his atonement in the repentance process.

A man appearing before a Church disciplinary council
grew angry when asked by the stake president to share his
innermost feelings about repentance. "What do my feelings
have to do with it, anyway?" he replied with disgust. "I have
done everything required of me to repent. I have completed
all of the steps of the repentance process. What more is there
for me to do? I have made a complete *confession,* made the
proper *restitution,* and *resolved* the matter. Isn't that repentance? My feelings are personal and are none of your business. They are irrelevant, since I have taken all of the steps
necessary to repent." This person also had focused his efforts
on a series of designated *actions* but rejected the notion that
genuine repentance also changes inward *attitudes.*

These true-to-life case studies are representative of
hundreds of examples of people, young and old, most with
good intentions and noble motives, who view repentance
merely as a series of steps to be taken or actions to be completed rather than an all-encompassing process of being,
changing, feeling, and doing. There are at least three serious
problems with trying to repent in this limited way.

First, under such a program a person may never really
"catch up." As one goes through the so-called requirements
of repentance, he will find that he has committed other sins

that also need his attention. To apply the "checklist" to every sin ever committed would be like taking one step forward and two steps backward. It would be impossible to conscientiously go through the process for every sin.

A second problem with such a process is that for some sins and situations there are not enough "Rs of repentance." For other sins there are items on the "checklist" that cannot be completed. President Spencer W. Kimball wrote that "there are some sins for which no adequate restitution can be made, and others for which only partial restitution is possible" (*The Miracle of Forgiveness* [Salt Lake City: Bookcraft, 1969], p. 194).

Finally, and most problematic of all, is that when we overemphasize "steps," or outward actions, we tend to elevate man's doings at the expense of Christ's cleansing power. We make repentance appear as though it is something that we can do by ourselves. Such a serious misconception minimizes the miraculous atonement of Jesus Christ and the grace of God that grants us forgiveness. When we focus all of our attention and effort on the things *we* must do to repent, we tend to overlook what *he* did to make repentance possible. Thus, the worst danger of this narrow view of repentance is that it all too often causes us to leave out the most important element, the most important "R" of repentance: *Redeemer.*

FAITH UNTO REPENTANCE

President Ezra Taft Benson has declared: "True repentance is based on and flows from faith in the Lord Jesus Christ. There is no other way" (*The Teachings of Ezra Taft Benson* [Salt Lake City: Bookcraft, 1988], p. 71). The scriptures — especially the Book of Mormon — contain many examples and teachings on faith as the first and foremost ingredient of repentance. After Enos spent an entire day praying for a witness of the truthfulness of his father's words, he was rewarded with a remission of his sins. When he asked, "Lord, how is it done?" The Lord taught him, "Because of thy faith in Christ, . . . thy faith hath made thee whole" (Enos 1:7–8). The terrible agony experienced by Alma the Younger, referred to earlier in this chapter, was relieved only when he remembered the teachings of his father concerning one Jesus Christ and his atonement. Even as he merely attempted to exercise faith in Christ, he suddenly and mercifully experienced the miracle of forgiveness.

"Now, as my mind caught hold upon this thought, I cried within my heart: O Jesus, thou Son of God, have mercy on me, who am in the gall of bitterness, and am encircled about by the everlasting chains of death.

"And now, behold, when I thought this, I could remember my pains no more; yea, I was harrowed up by the memory of my sins no more.

"And oh, what joy, and what marvelous light I did behold; yea, my soul was filled with joy as exceeding as was my pain!" (Alma 36:18–20).

A remission of sins was extended to Enos and Alma because they exercised faith in the atonement of Christ. Their abandonment of sinful practices, their restitution for past mistakes, and their continued commitment to the kingdom of God came afterward. These "steps" did not have to be accomplished in a certain order or be totally completed before forgiveness was granted. The "faith unto repentance" which these men exercised also led them to a natural desire to do the works of righteousness.

The prophet Amulek affirmed that faith must precede repentance for the mercy of the Messiah to be enjoyed.

"And thus he shall bring salvation to all those who shall believe on his name; this being the intent of this last sacrifice, to bring about the bowels of mercy, which overpowereth justice, and bringeth about means unto men that they may have *faith unto repentance.*

"And thus mercy can satisfy the demands of justice, and encircles them in the arms of safety, while he that exercises no *faith unto repentance* is exposed to the whole law of the demands of justice; therefore *only unto him that has faith unto repentance* is brought about the great and eternal plan of redemption" (Alma 34:15–15; emphasis added).

Truly, then, repentance stems only from faith in the redemptive and cleansing power of the blood of the Lamb of God. Without the merciful atonement there could be no forgiveness of our sins, no matter what *we* might do. Although there really is no set recipe or checklist of steps that must be taken in every case of repentance, we must still do all that we can, to demonstrate our faith. The Lord himself has given us no list of "Rs" to complete in the repentance process. Other than teaching that repentance begins with and flows from faith in Christ, he has given only this simple but important formula that includes all other actions and attitudes of repentance. He declared, "By this ye may know if a man repenteth of his sins—behold, he will confess them and forsake them" (D&C 58:43).

CONFESSION: ATTITUDES AND ACTIONS

As we see from this passage of scripture in the Doctrine and Covenants, confession is a sign of true repentance. Confession is much more than just admitting we have sinned, however. Sincere repentance requires an *attitude* of confession in the heart as well as an *action* of confession coming from the mouth. Whether it be a private, personal confession of sins, confession to priesthood leaders, or a more public confession to the Church congregation, the act of confession serves as an outward sign of what should be happening inside of us.

It would be hypocritical for us to confess our sins merely to complete one of the steps of repentance if we are not sincerely sorry for our wrongdoing. The kind of confession that will truly bring us forgiveness comes only from a deep sense of what the apostle Paul called "godly sorrow"—what the Book of Mormon refers to as "a broken heart and a contrite spirit" (2 Nephi 2:7). As Paul explained to the Corinthians, there is a difference between this righteous sorrowing and worldly sorrow. "Now I rejoice, not that ye were made sorry, but that ye sorrowed to repentance: for ye were made sorry after a godly manner. . . . For godly sorrow worketh repentance to salvation . . . but the sorrow of the world worketh death" (2 Corinthians 7:9). Being sorry, regretful, or remorseful does not by itself necessarily bring about repentance. We have probably all known persons who have been sorrowful and who have suffered for their mistakes but who have done nothing to change or to come unto Christ and comply with the requirements of the gospel. The "godly sorrow" of which Paul spoke arises from true faith in the Savior and not from a fear of being caught or punished. It is the only kind of sorrow which "worketh repentance to salvation."

How, then, do we know when the grief we feel because of our sins is "godly sorrow"? There are two important elements that are always a part of this righteous sorrowing.

An awful awareness of our unworthiness before God. Before sinners can obtain a remission of sins, they must experience what King Benjamin described as "an awful view of their own guilt and abominations, which doth cause them to shrink from the presence of the Lord" (Mosiah 3:25). If we do not even recognize our sins and don't see ourselves as we really are, how can we feel sorry? If we don't realize or care that our sins will separate us from God, how can we care about repenting? As Alma declared to his wayward son, Corianton: "Let your sins trouble you, with that trouble which shall bring you down unto repentance.... Do not endeavor to excuse yourself in the least point because of your sins, ... but do you let the justice of God, and his mercy, and his long-suffering have full sway in your heart; and let it bring you down to the dust in humility" (Alma 42:29–30). Accompanying the "awful awareness" of our unworthiness before the Lord is the yearning to be cleansed and to stand approved before him once again.

Willing submission and surrender to God's will for us. Perhaps one of the most important tests of godly sorrow is our willingness to submit to whatever the Lord requires of us in order to obtain a remission of our sins. It is not uncommon for some to desire to repent on their own terms rather than on the Lord's terms. They want to make repentance easy, pain-free, and convenient, when in reality it is sometimes difficult and demanding and may require some humiliation, public embarrassment, pain, restrictions, or inconvenience. It is not "godly sorrow" if a person—

• Confesses a major sin to the appropriate priesthood leader but is unwilling to follow the counsel or correction he or she receives.

• Procrastinates his confession and repentance until he gets into the mission field so he will not be embarrassed at home by having to wait a little longer before he can serve.

• Resents the restriction not to partake of the sacrament because he or she is worried about what others might think.

• Disguises the severity of the sin in confessing to the priesthood leader so he or she may gain admission to a Church-owned university or college.

President Spencer W. Kimball offered these questions as a way of determining the extent to which a person had repented and the depth of his or her conviction—

• Do you wish to be forgiven?

• Could you accept excommunication for the sin if deemed necessary?

• Why do you feel you should not be excommunicated?

• If you were, would you become bitter at the Church and its officers?

• Would you cease your activities in the Church?

• Would you work your way back to baptism and restoration of former blessings even through the years?

• Have you told your [spouse] or parents?

• Have you confessed your total sins?

• Are you humble now? Is your humility the result of "being forced to be humble?"

• Have you wrestled with your problems as did Enos?

• Has your soul hungered for your soul's sake?

(See *The Miracle of Forgiveness,* pp. 160–61).

If we possess the proper attitude of confession, our hearts will be broken with a piercing sorrow for sin and an "awful awareness" of our unworthiness. Our spirits will be humbled, and we will desire to submit to God's will and do whatever he requires to have the heavy burden of sin lifted from our shoulders.

A student once asked me this important question: "What can you do to feel that kind of godly sorrow? What if you don't feel genuinely sorry for your sins? Can you still repent?" As I pondered those questions, I could think of numerous people with whom I had counseled who really felt no remorse, let alone godly sorrow, for their sins. As I struggled with that dilemma, I learned that there really wasn't anything that I could do to bring them to that desired state. The Spirit testified to me that godly sorrow is a spiritual gift. It is bestowed upon us through our faith in Christ. In order to receive it, we must desire and pray for it with all our hearts, exercising faith in our Savior by whom it comes.

Once we have been blessed with the right attitude of confession, the appropriate action will naturally follow. "What sins must I confess?" and "To whom should I confess?" are questions commonly asked by young people. In the Book of Mormon, the Lord taught Alma that if a transgressor would "confess his sins before *thee* and *me,* and [repent] in the sincerity of his heart, him shall *ye* forgive, and *I* will forgive him also" (Mosiah 26:29; emphasis added). Perhaps we can better understand why we need to go both to the Lord *and* to his earthly priesthood authorities by learning why we are commanded to confess. Confession to the Lord and to the proper priesthood leader is not just telling them *what they need to know.* It is the expression of a commitment or the making of a covenant with them concerning *what we are going to do.* Just admitting our sins remains an incomplete confession unless it leads to two higher and more important purposes.

Confession as a covenant. For our own benefit, we disclose our deeds to the Lord, even though he already knows them, and to priesthood leaders, who may or may not know them. Such open acknowledgment of our evil actions demonstrates a spirit of humility and signals a desire to change. It gives us the chance to promise our Lord, our priesthood leader, and ourselves that we will make the necessary changes in our lives. This spoken promise, if sincere, will give us added power to help us reform our lives. Confession without a commitment to change is almost meaningless and will have little effect in helping us to repent fully.

Confession as an opportunity to receive direction. Confessing sins to friends, roommates, or even family members may seem helpful at first. There may be a temporary lifting of the heavy burden of guilt, but this feeling is fleeting. The lasting healing of both mind and spirit can come only from the Great Physician himself—Jesus Christ. When we come unto Christ through a complete confession and a commitment to change our ways, we are then in a position to be taught by the Master. His guidance far surpasses any emotional support or well-meant advice from mere mortals. In addition, his inspired servants—the common judges in Israel (bishops, branch presidents, mission presidents, and stake and district presidents)—have been ordained and set apart to a special stewardship that qualifies them alone to lift the burdens of those who confess major sins and to forgive them in behalf of the Church. It is for these reasons that the Lord requires that a confession be made to judges in Israel for moral transgressions and other serious sins. That procedure is not designed to punish or humiliate us. These authorized leaders, regardless of their background or station in life, represent our Savior and by inspiration can provide the repentant sinner with the counsel, direction, and the discipline needed for full repentance.

Thus, once we have acquired a sincere *attitude* of repentance and an understanding of and a desire for the blessings and help that can come to us through the *action* of confession, we will begin to see confession as more than a "step" to be completed on our checklist. We will not need a "list" of sins that require formal confession. Instead, we will be prompted by the workings of the Spirit and by our own need to be forgiven to approach the proper priesthood leader, as necessary, in humble confession and to seek his counsel and support. Our confession to others whom we may also have wronged should also be guided by the whisperings of the Holy Ghost and the counsel of priesthood leaders. If we are truly repentant, we will be willing to be obedient to these promptings and such counsel, doing *all* that we can to be forgiven rather than searching for some less demanding course.

FORSAKING SIN: "THE MIGHTY CHANGE"

Through the attitude of confession—a manifestation of godly sorrow—we open the gate; through the action of confession, we step onto the "strait and narrow path" leading to forgiveness; however, repentance is not yet complete without fulfilling the second requirement in the Lord's formula—forsaking sin. As important as confession is, the final and most telling test of true repentance is in the way we live our lives after our confession.

Forsaking sin is all too often misunderstood to mean that one merely stops committing the particular sin of which he or she is repenting; however, the Lord's definition of forsaking sin implies the abandonment of sinfulness in every aspect of our lives and character. Consider the incompleteness of repentance in the following two examples:

1. A young man confesses a sexual transgression to his priesthood leader and promises never again to fall into that sin, but he continues to drink and use illegal drugs.

2. A college student confesses a sin of shoplifting. She

forsakes that sin of stealing, seeks the forgiveness of the Lord
and of the person offended, and pays back the monetary value
of the items taken. But she deliberately continues to gossip,
backbite, and criticize other ward members.

In each of these examples, it is apparent that although
these individuals may have forsaken one specific sin, they
really have not yet changed their tendencies and desires to
sin. Each has attempted to give up one sin while clinging
tightly to others. Such half-hearted repentance will have little
power to keep them from falling back into their former sins.
Forsaking, like confessing, comprises attitudes as well as actions. It is not just the abandonment of an action—it is the
changing of one's entire being. Alma called the acquisition
of this kind of attitude a "mighty change in your hearts"
(Alma 5:14).

Like "godly sorrow," the "mighty change of heart" comes
to us as a gift through the grace and mercy of Jesus Christ.
Nevertheless, the scriptures and the prophets of God have
declared that we are able to receive this gift of a "new heart"
(Ezekiel 36:26) only through the exercise of our faith as we
demonstrate our sincere repentance.

As we strive to be worthy of this gift, perhaps we should
consider some other "Rs" of repentance that must not be
overlooked. There must be a *reeducation* of our minds, a
reordering of our priorities, a *redirecting* of our desires, and a
reshaping of our characters. President Spencer W. Kimball
further taught that forsaking sin may also require a change
of friends and associations, a change of circumstances and
environments. He then reminded us that "it is not a simple
matter for one to transform his life overnight, nor to change
attitudes in a moment, nor to rid himself in a hurry of un-

worthy companions" ("What Is True Repentance?" *New Era,*
May 1974, p. 7).

Repentance is a serious, demanding, and continuing process. We cannot do it halfway and expect complete forgiveness. We must not attempt to be on both sides of the imaginary line between good and evil. "Ye cannot serve God and
mammon," declared Jesus (Matthew 6:24). Such divided loyalties block the development of the faith needed to receive
the "mighty change of heart" that will lead us to forsake our
sins. We cannot, figuratively speaking, have one hand reaching for the fruit of the "tree of life" while continuing to dance
and dine in the "great and spacious building," for it requires
both hands and our whole heart and soul to cling to the "iron
rod" (1 Nephi 11:8–36).

As we make the necessary changes required for true repentance, we will be worthy of the "new heart" that only the
Lord can bestow on us. Often we struggle mightily, trying to
overcome our sins through our own efforts alone. We may
feel overwhelmed and frustrated and hopelessly unable to
change when we think we must rely on our own puny human
willpower. We can never achieve repentance in this way, but
if through our faith and works we are endowed with the
"mighty change" of heart, we will find the desire to have evil
purged from us by the power of the Holy Ghost and we will
also enjoy greater power to do good.

Indeed, forsaking evil includes not only refraining from
sin but also a new determination to do righteous works. In
the true spirit of repentance, it is not enough simply to cleanse
a filthy vessel. The cleansed vessel must then be filled with
a pure substance to ensure that it is not contaminated again.
The Savior taught a parable that illustrates this principle—

"When the unclean spirit is gone out of a man, he walketh

through dry places, seeking rest; and finding none, he saith, I will return unto my house whence I came out.

"And when he cometh, he findeth it swept and garnished.

"Then goeth he, and taketh to him seven other spirits more wicked than himself; and they enter in, and dwell there: and the last state of that man is worse than the first" (Luke 11:24–26).

Although the "house" had been swept or cleansed, the evil spirit took more spirits like himself and returned to the unoccupied house and reentered it. In a similar way, our lives may be like the empty house after our sins are swept away. We remain open to a reinvasion of all manner of temptations and trouble if our lives are not filled with renewed acts of righteousness, greater devotion to God, and increased service to others. We must become so filled with goodness that there is not room for our "former sins [to] return" (D&C 82:7). As Elder Boyd K. Packer counseled: "Do not try merely to *discard* a bad habit or a bad thought. *Replace* it. When you try to eliminate a bad habit, if the spot where it used to be is left open it will sneak back and crawl again into that empty space. It grew there; it will struggle to stay there. . . . Replace it with unselfish thoughts, with unselfish acts. Then, if an evil habit or addiction tries to return, it will have to fight for attention. . . . You are in charge of you. I repeat, it is very, very difficult to eliminate a bad habit [or sin] just by trying to discard it. Replace it" (*"That All May Be Edified"* [Salt Lake City: Bookcraft, 1982], p. 196).

Thus, *forsaking* means not only turning away from sin but also turning back to God, keeping his commandments, serving our fellowmen, and doing all that we can to pay our debt to the Savior, whose marvelous atonement made it possible for us to be made clean again and to once again enjoy a soul at peace.

PREVENTION IS BETTER THAN REDEMPTION

We are most blessed to have this great gift of forgiveness available to us when we make mistakes. Yet some people actually believe that in some ways they are better off because they "sowed their wild oats." These people often feel that by virtue of their "experience" they may be better able to empathize with and help those who are struggling to repent of sin. Others may feel that they appreciate and understand the Atonement better by having needed its cleansing power so desperately. Still others claim that they could have learned certain important lessons only in the "hard knocks" school of sin. These are all mistaken ideas about repentance. Though we teach and testify of the glorious blessings associated with repentance, we cannot neglect the even greater blessings that flow from obedience and continued righteousness. "The more I see of life," stated President Harold B. Lee, "the more I am convinced that we must impress you young people with the awfulness of sin rather than to content ourselves with merely teaching the way of repentance" (*Decisions for Successful Living* [Salt Lake City: Deseret Book Co., 1973], p. 88).

We must always bear in mind that there are blessings and opportunities that come from steadfast faith, obedience, and continued good works that we may lose during seasons of inactivity or sinful behavior. Even though we repent and are forgiven, opportunities for growth and spiritual development may be lost to us. For this reason, President Spencer W. Kimball stated: "Prevention is far better than redemption" (in Conference Report, Oct. 1977, p. 34). The blessings of obedience and the rewards for righteousness are far greater than the results of repeated repentance.

One subtle and successful strategy used by the adversary is to convince Latter-day Saint youth that since we are blessed with the possibility of repentance, we have a spiritual safety net to catch us whenever we choose to fall. There are many dangerous pitfalls in this way of thinking, however. A person who *plans* to sin and then to repent mocks the Atonement and may find sincere repentance much more difficult than he imagined; partly because he has felt that he can use the sacred Atonement for his own selfish purposes—a serious sin in itself. Moreover, if he repents to meet his own timetable (that is, for a mission, for temple marriage, etc.), rather than because of genuine godly sorrow, he might think he has been forgiven because he has completed certain "steps" of repentance, when in truth, he has not exercised real "faith unto repentance." Finally, sinfulness—whether it be an extended relationship with worldliness or a brief flirtation with iniquity—has its own long-term consequences that may continue even after we have received forgiveness. Some of these include regret that stays with us all of our lives, the loss of blessings and opportunities, and even the possibility of becoming so depraved that we lose the will or capacity to repent at all.

A Lifetime of Regret

Recounting his conversion, Alma the Younger said:

"And now, for three days and for three nights was I racked, even with the pains of a damned soul.

"And it came to pass that as I was thus racked with torment, while I was harrowed up by the memory of my many sins, behold, I remembered also to have heard my father prophesy unto the people concerning the coming of one Jesus Christ, a Son of God, to atone for the sins of the world.

"Now, as my mind caught hold upon this thought, I cried within my heart: O Jesus, thou Son of God, have mercy on me, who am in the gall of bitterness, and am encircled about by the everlasting chains of death.

"And now, behold, when I thought this, I could remember my pains no more; yea, I was harrowed up by the memory of my sins no more.

"And oh, what joy, and what marvelous light I did behold; yea, my soul was filled with joy as exceeding as was my pain!

"Yea, I say unto you, my son, that there could be nothing so exquisite and so bitter as were my pains. Yea, and again I say unto you, my son, that on the other hand, there can be nothing so exquisite and sweet as was my joy" (Alma 36:16–21).

That is the blessing of repentance—the anguish of sin can be swallowed up in the joy of forgiveness. But even though we may find the peace of conscience and the joy that accompany a remission of sins, the memory of our sins does not necessarily leave us in this life. That is particularly true where our sinful behavior may have adversely affected or influenced others. For instance, consider parents whose poor example may have been partly responsible for the lack of spirituality or for the inactivity of one or more of their children. Even though the parents may ultimately repent, embrace the gospel, perhaps go the the temple, and even become a powerful force for good in the Church, in light of the effect their poor example has had on their children's attitude, how do you suppose mom and dad will view their former sins?

A student in one of my religion classes at BYU described that kind of lingering regret. This student granted permission for me to use his experience anonymously to help others realize that even repentance cannot wipe out all the "side effects" of sin. He wrote:

"I have come to a personal awareness of the effects of the Atonement in my life, but it is a bittersweet awareness. I have learned that neither repentance nor forgiveness is free or simple. I rejoice greatly in the peace I have found. I know in a measure the feeling of having my guilt swept away, and I will be eternally grateful for the extent of the Savior's love for me. But I sorrow that this awareness came as it did.

"Sinning, with the idea of repenting later, is such an easy deception to fall into. This attitude makes it seem like you can have the world's fun and enjoyment—do the things you are commanded not to do—as long as you plan to repent. The fallacy is in thinking that when you do repent, all is forgotten. But there are things lost that cannot be regained. After the process is complete (repenting and being forgiven), the guilt and pain are taken away but regret remains—regret at having sinned. I find for me that as my love and under-standing of the Savior and his love increase, so does my regret. I regret having knowingly done that which was not right. I regret having wasted so much time and stifling my progres-sion. But more and more, I have regret for the suffering that a loving Brother endured, suffering for my sins, suffering because of my selfishness.

"Beyond regret—even in forgiveness, all is not restored as at first. When we sin against a greater light, the light in us is darkened, and that kind of darkness stains the mind and soul. It is easy to fall into a hole, but even after you repent and are forgiven, you still have to climb out, and that climb can be a long hard process. The stains of darkness take a lot of scrubbing to be completely removed.

"Some people imagine that you have to 'taste the bitter,' or that certain experiences will make them a better person. But sinning is full of deception, and much of what a person 'learns' through sinning must later be 'unlearned.'

"Forgiveness is a wonderful reality and a glorious hope. But nothing, no willful misuse of free agency for either momentary pleasure or the satisfaction of curiosity, can compensate for that which is lost. Whether all can be replaced eventually, I don't know, but the process of climbing back up to where we were, the process of cleansing the 'stains' of darkness (even after the darkness is gone), the process of catching up to where you could have been, is a constant struggle, a great effort, and takes time that could have been spent basking in a greater light and a greater peace. You have to win battles that were better off not fought."

Loss of Blessings and Opportunities

In addition to the painful regrets, there are also blessings and opportunities for growth and service that are lost because of sinful vacations taken from living the gospel. President Harold B. Lee taught: "But now, please do not misunderstand. . . . One may not wallow in the mire of filth and sin and conduct his life in a manner unlawful in the sight of God and then suppose that repentance will wipe out the effects of his sin and place him on the level he would have been on had he always lived a righteous and virtuous life. . . . The Lord extends loving mercy and kindness in forgiving you of the sins you commit against him or his work, *but he can never remove the results of the sin you have committed against yourselves by thus retarding your advancement toward your eternal goal*" (*Decisions for Successful Living*, p. 100; emphasis added).

Thus, we are never better off for having sinned.

The Savior's greatness and his expansive spiritual character were the consequences of righteousness, not the fruits of repentance. We lose blessings through disobedience and sin and gain blessings through faithfulness and obedience. Believing that sinning and eventually repenting yield important experience or knowledge is also a false idea. Groveling in the gutters of wickedness may make us "streetwise" in worldly ways, but such knowledge does not compare to the "intelligence, or, in other words, light and truth" which is the "glory of God" (D&C 93:36). Feeling that we can better understand and strengthen other sinners because of our shared experience is also a well-intended but mistaken idea. Such understanding is not the same as the compassion for sinners that comes only from charity—"the pure love of Christ"—a spiritual gift that God bestows "upon all who are true followers of his Son, Jesus Christ" (Moroni 7:47–48).

For these reasons we cannot go back and do the good we failed to do, anymore than we can undo all of the harm that may have been caused by our evil actions. On the other hand, righteousness and continued obedience enlarge our capacities and expand our opportunities to contribute to the building of the kingdom. "What adventure in that great and spacious building would you trade," asked Bishop Glenn L. Pace of the Presiding Bishopric, "for the thrill and excitement of building the very kingdom the Savior will come to the earth to govern?" ("They're Not Really Happy," *Ensign,* Nov. 1987, p. 41).

For those who have already strayed from the "strait and narrow" and who have lost blessings and opportunities they might have had, it is not too late. Do not focus on what you have lost; focus on what you may still accomplish. Sometimes repentant sinners work so diligently and steadily to make up lost ground that they may actually surpass those Saints who have never wandered far from the path but who have never "lengthened their stride," either.

Loss of Desire or Power to Repent

The Book of Mormon prophet Amulek cautioned against putting off the day of repentance, warning the people of the binding power of sin: "For behold, if ye have procrastinated the day of your repentance . . . ," he warned, "ye have become subjected to the spirit of the devil, and he doth seal you his; therefore, the Spirit of the Lord hath withdrawn from you, and hath no place in you, and the devil hath all power over you" (Alma 34:35). Although the Savior stands with open arms of mercy and beckons us to repent, we must never selfishly think that we can return to him whenever we like, for we may discover the sad truth that President Spencer W. Kimball has described: "Sin is intensely habit-forming and sometimes moves men to the tragic point of no return. . . . As the transgressor moves deeper and deeper in his sin, and the error is entrenched more deeply and the will to change is weakened, it becomes increasingly near-hopeless, and he skids down and down until either he does not want to climb back or he has lost the power to do so" (*The Miracle of Forgiveness*, p. 117).

STAYING ON THE LORD'S SIDE OF THE LINE

How can we be sure that we will never reach that "tragic point of no return"? How can we avoid the regret and the loss of blessings and opportunities? Perhaps the answer to all of these questions is found in the inspired words of President Ezra Taft Benson: "It is better to prepare and prevent than it is to repair and repent. The first line of defense . . . is to prepare ourselves to resist temptation and prevent ourselves from falling into sin" ("The Law of Chastity," *BYU Speeches of the Year* [Provo, Utah: Brigham Young University Press, 1987–88], p. 51). To do that, we must be constantly watchful as well as prayerful to ensure that our thoughts, words, and deeds stay in a spiritual "safe zone." President George Albert Smith spoke of the safety found in keeping ourselves on "the Lord's side of the line":

"My grandfather used to say to his family, 'There is a line of demarcation, well defined, between the Lord's territory and the devil's. If you will stay on the Lord's side of the line you will be under his influence and will have no desire to do wrong; but if you cross to the devil's side of the line one inch, you are in the tempter's power, and if he is successful, you will not be able to think or even reason properly, because you will have lost the spirit of the Lord.'

"When I have been tempted sometimes to do a certain thing, I have asked myself, 'Which side of the line am I on?' If I determined to be on the safe side, the Lord's side, I would do the right thing every time. So when temptation comes think prayerfully about your problem, and the influence of the Spirit of the Lord will enable you to decide wisely. There is safety for us only on the Lord's side of the line" (*Sharing the Gospel with Others* [Salt Lake City: Deseret Book Co., 1948], pp. 42–43).

Where do we get the strength to resist temptation and stay on the Lord's side of the line? Such strength, like repentance, godly sorrow, the mighty change of heart, and charity, comes to us through faith in the Lord, Jesus Christ. The prophet Alma counseled his son Helaman, who was about to embark on a mission, to teach the people "an everlasting hatred against sin and iniquity. . . . Teach them to withstand every temptation of the devil, with their faith on the Lord Jesus Christ" (Alma 37:32–33). Such faith will naturally lead us to do many of the other things required to help us resist temptation—humble ourselves, "watch and pray continually, that [we] may not be tempted above that which [we] can bear, and thus be led by the Holy Spirit" (Alma 13:28), keep the commandments, serve others, and love God with all our hearts.

REPENTANCE IS A LIFELONG PROCESS

From all that we have discussed, it is obvious that repentance is not simple, easy, or quick. Whether our sins be serious or small, we are never finished repenting. As we strive to keep moving in our lifelong journey of repentance and obedience, though at times it may seem like climbing a spiritual Mount Everest, the words of King Benjamin are important to remember. He cautioned that a person should not "run faster than he has strength" (Mosiah 4:27). The Lord does not expect us to attempt to do more than we can—or to be perfect right now. He does desire that we diligently and steadily keep moving in the right direction, doing our own individual best. Elder B. H. Roberts, a general authority in the early days of the Church, noted, "It is by resisting temptation today, overcoming a weakness tomorrow, forsaking evil associations the next day, and thus day by day, month after month, year after year, pruning, restraining and weeding out that which is evil in the disposition, that the character is purged of its imperfections" (*Gospel and Man's Relationship to Deity* [Salt Lake City: Deseret Book Co., 1965], pp. 197–98).

Even as we do all we can to reach perfection one step at a time, we will never be expected to achieve perfection on our own. Our Savior will once again do for us that which we cannot do for ourselves. For if we "come unto Christ," he will ultimately perfect us by the grace of God, "through the shedding of the blood of Christ" (Moroni 10:32–33).

I testify of the cleansing power of the blood of Christ. I have experienced in my own life the mercy and love of Jesus Christ and have witnessed the steady as well as the spectacular changes wrought in the lives of others through God's gift of repentance. Heavy hearts are lifted and sin-seared souls are miraculously healed by the Great Physician. Sins that are "as scarlet" can truly become as white as newly fallen snow.

INDEX